To Don !
Best Wishes !
Jerome Att

Oh, Hard Tuesday

A Novella

Jerome Arthur

.

Oh, Hard Tuesday

Published by Jerome Arthur
P.O. Box 818
Santa Cruz, California 95061
831-425-8818
www.JeromeArthurNovelist.com
Jerome@JeromeArthurNovelist.com

Dedicated to
the memory of
Don Rothman and Morton Marcus

Acknowledgments

Thanks to Robert Yonts, Christina George and Todd Newberry for editorial assistance, and Sherri Goodman for the cover design

One

Danielle Bourdain was sitting at my desk going over the report I had put together on her niece. She'd contacted me a few days earlier, recommended by Jayne Smith, a client whose missing husband I'd located in Baja California the previous April. My office was in a little California bungalow that was also my home on Center Street in Downtown Santa Cruz. The place was tiny, about 600 square feet. It had three small rooms, a kitchen and a bathroom. The smallest room, which was my office, was only big enough to hold a small desk, a two-drawer file cabinet and two armless chairs, one for me and one for the client. She had put the report back on the desk. As we stood up, I tucked it into a manila envelope and handed it to her.

"Well, Jack," she said. "Right now, I'm going home, and I'm go'n'a watch the ball game with Jason. Not even go'n'a think about this tonight."

"Good idea."

As we headed to the front door, all hell broke loose. The house started rocking violently back and forth. This was really a big earthquake. Danielle and I had just passed through the door separating my office from the living room. I put my arm around her shoulder and backed up so that she was standing in the doorway, then only one step for me over to the doorway of the room at the front of the house, my bedroom. My bookcase with the C.D. player and receiver on top was next to that door, so I held it steady with my left arm while hugging the doorjamb with my right. Out the front window, the power lines were swinging like jump ropes. Aside from the noise of everything falling out of the refrigerator and a cabinet crashing against the hot water tank in the service porch, the sound that pervaded was a low roar coming from who knows where? Danielle and I were both speechless. She held tight to the envelope with the report in it. The movement continued for what seemed like minutes, but in real time was only seventeen seconds. When it ended, we stepped out of the two doorways into the middle of the living room.

"Wow! What a ride that was!" I said.

The electricity was off and there was a slight smell of gas in the air. Some books had tumbled out of the bookcase and were scattered on the floor. I stepped over them to the kitchen counter and saw the open refrigerator. The mayonnaise and mustard jars were broken on the floor in front of it. Mixed in with that mess was the almost full half-gallon carton of chocolate milk, which broke wide open on impact.

"I've got'a go." This was Danielle. I'd almost forgotten her in all the chaos.

Saying no more, she turned and went out the front door. Her car was parked in front, so she went right to it, got in and drove away. Not five minutes after she left, the street was a traffic jam. It was a slow-moving parking lot.

As soon as she was gone, I went to the service porch, got my crescent wrench, went out to the gas meter by the front porch, and shut the gas off. Then I went next door to see how Lil was and to shut her gas off, too. Lil ran a barber shop out of her house. We had a kind of little home business row on our block. There were only two of us, so I guess that counts as a row. Maybe it was more like we were twins. Her house, like mine, was still on its foundation. It was a Spanish stucco, red tile roof, hacienda-style house about the same size as mine. She was pacing on her front porch. Her gas meter was in front of the house just like mine.

"I'll shut your gas off here, Lil," I said as I did the job. "You okay?"

"…think so…little shook up is all…just finished my last haircut for the day…worried about his own place…shot outa' here without paying…everything's okay here, I think…."

She *was* shook up. Babbling and fretting. Probably in shock for the second time in three days. Her house was broken into early Sunday morning and she got knocked around by the intruder. She still had traces of a black eye, and the cut on her forehead hadn't healed yet.

"Go back inside. Lie down."

I set the crescent wrench down by her front door and followed her in. She went straight to her bedroom.

"Right behind yuh, babe."

9

Oh, Hard Tuesday

"Oh, good." Her voice was barely audible.

Her shop was in the front room. There was still hair on the floor around her chair. I walked through it and into her bedroom. She was lying on top of the covers shivering. Lil was in her fifties, still a very beautiful woman for her age at about five-four and a hundred forty pounds. She wore a medium length tinted blond hairstyle that set off her blue eyes. Her skin was velvety smooth, and she always dressed to the nines. She was still wearing the orthopedic shoes and the smock she wore behind the barber chair. She liked to wear skirts to show off her shapely legs and low-cut blouses that highlighted her equally shapely bosoms.

"Okay, Lil, you're go'n'a have to sit up here for a minute. Take your shoes and smock off and get under the covers."

After I tucked her in, I went to the kitchen and got her a glass of water. I held the glass and helped her drink, and then she lay back down and said she wanted to rest. She had a mess in front of her refrigerator too, so I cleaned it up as best I could, and went back in the bedroom and checked on her. She seemed to be resting peacefully. I went back to my place.

I surveyed my property for the next fifteen minutes, putting things back in place and generally restoring order. Nothing happened to the garage, which was just a shed with a dirt floor and no foundation. Go figure. The rest of the property seemed to be in fairly good shape for the age of the structure. No major damage. I was thankful that the redwood tree on the rear property line didn't fall into the house. Redwood trees are no doubt used to earthquakes. After all, they do live along the fault line in the northern part of the state. The mess on my kitchen floor was going to have to wait because I wanted to go over and check out the Mall before they closed it off, which I was sure would be soon.

After making sure my house was okay, I locked the place up, and took a walk over to the Pacific Garden Mall, the main drag in downtown Santa Cruz, two blocks behind my place. This was a bustling six-block stretch of hundred-year-old commercial buildings along a one-way street with wide sidewalks and bench-high planter boxes and shade trees. It had been converted from a two-way street with narrow sidewalks and traffic signals into a mall twenty years ago. It was like walking in a well-manicured garden when you strolled from one end to the other, and what a shock it was to see it now. Trees had fallen into storefronts and the street. It was so obliterated; you had to climb over trees and rubble to get through. There was red dust in the air everywhere, all from the many unreinforced brick buildings that had been built after the fire in the late 1800s.

Four guys inside the Ford's store were moving bricks and other debris away from the adjoining wall with an old building called Hotel Metropole, which housed Plaza Books/Paper Vision. The front plate glass window was blown out, so I stepped over more debris to see what they were doing. One of the guys saw me coming.

"Give us a hand here! There're people underneath all this!"

Oh, Hard Tuesday

So, I went in through the window and started to help.

Two

The earthquake was the worst disaster I ever lived through, the hardest Tuesday of my life. Before that the worst was the flood in December of '55 before the Army Corps of Engineers built the levee. I was a teenager when that one came down. I heard one story about how a guy rowed a boat the mile and a half from downtown to the beach on Ocean Street. My little home office, long before I lived there, was two feet under water. Another bad flood happened in January of '82, after the levee. Water was up to my threshold in that one. Fortunately, none of it got into the house. Lil took on about three inches inside her place. Half of the Soquel Bridge was taken out when it became a dam after logs and other debris backed up on the north side of it. Same thing for the Riverside Avenue Bridge. But none of that was anything compared to the Loma Prieta earthquake in 1989. We literally lost the entire downtown business district. Watsonville, which was closer to the epicenter, got it worse.

Five days before the quake, Danielle Bourdain hired me to find her missing niece, Karen Babbit, a U.C. Santa Cruz senior. Danielle had gotten my name from her friend Jayne Smith. Jayne had hired me in April to find her husband, who, one day out of the blue, up and disappeared, only leaving a note telling her he was going away, but not telling her where, or when, or even *if* he'd be coming back. It took me two weeks to find him in Santa Rosalil-lita down in Baja California. After she got my report, she and Danielle drove down to Baja, and found him where I told her he was.

When Danielle came through my door, I was struck by her obvious, but understated beauty. She looked to be in her early forties. She wore no make-up, didn't need to. She had soft olive skin, a dimple in her chin, and dark eyes with long, curved-up lashes. Her thick, shoulder-length, black hair was tied back. She wore blue denim jeans, not too tight, and a loose-fitting T-shirt that said, "Save the Whales" across the front. If she hadn't been so pretty, she might have looked just plain. She made me think of pictures I'd seen of Joan Baez when she first came into the public eye.

I didn't get much of a chance to show my astonishment at her good looks. She did a double take when she looked at me.

"Boy, you *do* look like James Garner, don't you?" she said as we shook hands.

"I guess so," I said. "A lot of people tell me that. You sound forewarned."

"Jayne told me about the resemblance, and she was right."

"So, what exactly can I help you with?"

"I have a niece who's a senior at U.C. Santa Cruz, and I think she's missing. I was hoping you'd be able to find her."

"Have you talked to the police?" I said.

"Actually, no. I'd like to keep this confidential. I really don't think she's in any danger. Just missing."

"How long's it been since your last contact with her?"

"I spoke to her on the phone in early September, before the start of the fall quarter, but I haven't been able to reach her since. Last time I tried was Monday. Her answering machine was full, not taking any new messages. Last time I saw her was around when Jayne and I left for México before school got out in June."

"You should call the police. They've got better resources than I. Plus, they'll do it for you for free. Or at least you've already paid for it with your taxes."

"I don't want to involve the police."

This made me wary. My first thought was that Danielle wasn't telling me everything. What could she possibly be hiding?

"I'm not worried about the money. I'd just like to find out what happened to Karen. When we talked in early September, she sounded really up about the coming quarter. Excited to be getting back to finish her last year of college."

"Have you talked to her friends, her parents?"

"Yes. Talked to her parents on the phone last night. I called them after I spoke to her friend Lisa Hughes yesterday afternoon. Those two girls were roommates on campus. Karen's had a room at the Palomar since last year. Lisa said she's in two classes with her this quarter, and Karen hasn't showed up for either of them. School's been in session for almost a month now. Lisa says she checked with the teacher of Karen's third class, and she hasn't been there, either. She's been trying to reach Karen by phone, too. Left several messages; she doesn't return her calls. Now she says she gets a recorded message that her mailbox is full. Same response I got on Monday. I even tried her door a couple times before I went home after work. No answer. My sister and her husband saw her last June right after I saw her. She went home for a week at the end of spring quarter. Came back to town because she had a job for the summer down here. Or so she said."

"How close is she with her parents?"

"They've tried to call her a couple times, and they haven't been able to reach her, either. I don't think they're a close family. I don't know. Jayne's on the phone a lot with her daughter, Caroline, since she's been away at school. I don't think my sister and her husband call Karen much. Not like that, anyway. I might be closer to her than they are. But they *are* concerned."

"You say she's got a room at the Palomar, right?"

"Yes. Lived on campus the first two years. Rented the room at the Palomar Inn last year. Said she'd be staying there till she graduates. I've knocked on her door a couple times this summer, but she hasn't been there. I checked with the management, and they say they haven't seen her for quite a while."

"She got a boyfriend?"

"She's talked about a boy named Jason, but I never got the impression there was anything romantic between them. I remember the name because it's the same as my husband's. Karen, Lisa and Jason were in the dorm at College Eight. The way she talked about him, it was more like they were study partners. But I don't know."

"She get good grades? Good student?"

"I think so. You know how when these kids get out on their own, they don't share a lot of stuff with an old aunt. I'm sure she's an excellent student."

"Okay," I said as I finished writing some rough notes down in my notebook. "I want you to start with Karen's name and contact info. Then we can go down the list of all her friends and how I can get in touch with them. If you know any others to contact: her faculty advisor, teachers, let me get them down, too. Do you have a picture of Karen?"

She opened her wallet, took a picture out and handed it to me. It was a tight shot, waist up, of Danielle and another beautiful, lighter complexioned brunette, only younger and with blue eyes. She had the same dimpled chin as her aunt. The scene looked like West Cliff Drive, its ocean-sky-horizon in the background. I set it aside and started writing out the list in my notebook. It was sparse. She gave me Karen's name, phone number and address first. Lisa Hughes and Jason (no last name) were next, and only Lisa had a phone. Danielle told me to make a note under Jason's name that I could get his last name and number from Lisa. The next name under Jason's was Rebecca Ginsberg. No phone number, but once again a note that I could get it from Lisa. That was it. No adviser, no other teachers. It looked like I was going to have to rely on Lisa for any more information.

I got one of my standard contracts out of the file cabinet and filled in the blanks. She signed it and wrote me a check. She stood up and offered her hand.

"Thank you," she said. "I hope you can find out something. This isn't like her. She's never done anything like this before."

"I'm sure she hasn't. Who is Rebecca Ginsberg?"

"Another friend of Karen's. I think she might be older than Karen. Maybe already graduated."

"Okay. This is a pretty sparse list. I'll do what I can with it."

"You know how it is. A young girl goes off to college, tries to make the break from her family. Karen and I have an excellent relationship, but she really *is* trying to gain her independence."

"I'll get busy on this right away."

"Thank you. I appreciate any help you can give my sister and me."

We shook hands and she left. I looked at the list of names she'd given me.

Three

Looking at the meager list, I could see clearly that this was going to require a call to Jean Kaiser at the P.D. Jean was a good friend I'd known since high school. There was never any romance between us, but we did go to the senior prom together, and we always flirted with each other going back to before the prom. She'd gone to Cabrillo College where she got a two-year degree in Administration of Justice and joined the P.D. as a spokesperson for the department. She was my first inspiration to pick up my A.J. certificate at Cabrillo. Because of our special relationship, Jean was usually good to check out people for me, but she had to do it on the sly. Her boss, Lieutenant Jenkins, frowned on her doing those kinds of favors for me. I think he was a bit jealous of our relationship. I guess he thought there was something romantic going on, which there wasn't. It was strictly platonic with a little flirting here and there.

The day was young, and I wanted to go surfing before it was over. Low tide was a couple hours off. The best time to get in the water at Cowell's was about an hour before low tide. I started surfing that break when Jayne hired me to find Soc. Since it was his favorite break, it was one of the first places I went to get information about him from his surfing buddies. The waves there were small, and you stayed up for a long time after you made your drop, what little drop there was. Four Mile used to be my favorite break, but after just one session at Cowell's, I was a convert. I wasn't crazy about big surf anymore.

Danielle had come to my office during her lunch hour from a nearby preschool where she worked. Not having any other cases at the time, I got to work on hers right away. I had a couple things to do before I could get ready to go surfing, like call Lisa Hughes. Her answering machine picked up, so I left a message with my name and phone number and asked her to call me back. Jean was my next call.

"Hey, doll. What's up?"

While a lot of people in Santa Cruz were being politically correct, Jean and I weren't having any of it. I called her "doll" all the time and she loved it. She was crazy about the post-World-War-Two era when the "fella's" called their women friends "doll."

"Mr. Lefevre," she said, being proper and professional. In a more casual setting she would've said, "Hi there, big fella'," or at least called me by my first name.

"Since you used my last name, may I assume that you're not alone?"

"Yes, you may. I'm in the middle of something right now. I'll call you back in about ten minutes?"

"You know the number."

"By heart."

"I'll let you go. Call me when you get a chance."

And we broke the connection. I finished writing a report for an insurance company investigation I'd just completed. The phone rang.

"Jack Lefevre."

"Hello, Mr. Lefevre," came a young woman's voice. "This is Lisa Hughes."

"Oh, hi. Glad you called me back. I'd like to talk to you about Karen Babbit. Her aunt Danielle says she's missing, and she's concerned. Said you haven't seen her lately, either."

"Right. Like how can I help?"

"I'd rather not discuss it over the phone. Perhaps we could meet somewhere and talk about it."

"Sure. Like I'm not busy right now. Yuh wan'a like come over here?"

"That sounds good. Where do you live?"

"Like I've got a room in the Abbott row houses on Lincoln Street downtown."

"I'll be there in ten minutes. I'm just around the corner."

She gave me her address. I gathered up my pen and notebook and walked the two blocks to her place.

Standing on the front porch was a petite, brown-eyed young woman with long brown hair tied back in a ponytail dressed in Levi jeans and a pink blouse. She was cute. She had a bit of an acne problem, but it didn't detract from her cuteness.

"Lisa?" I said walking up to the porch.

"Yes. Are you like Mr. Lefevre?"

"Not just 'like' him, but the genuine article, the real deal."

"Come in," she said. "Like this is actually a good time. My roommates are home and they know Karen, too."

The row houses were old. They had a blue plaque identifying them as historical houses. She opened the front door and I followed her in. The décor was perennial college student. Thumb-tacked to one wall was a poster of Tom Petty and the Heartbreakers on stage with Bob Dylan. On the opposite wall was another poster, this one a picture of Jesse Jackson, from the shoulders-up, smiling in front of an American flag. A two-line caption at the bottom read, "Jesse Jackson for President/1988." A rainbow arched over the date. There were a threadbare couch and chair that didn't match. No television. There was a staircase on the wall to the right, leading to the bedrooms. The kitchen was at the rear of the unit on the other side of an informal dining area. A door led out to a small backyard.

The two roommates were sitting at the table, which was scattered with books and papers. As we approached, they gathered the papers up and closed the books.

"Mr. Lefevre, these are my roommates, Diana and Lucy."

Diana had blue eyes and long blond hair tied back like Lisa. She was wearing Jordache jeans and a T-shirt with a logo that said, "Take Back the Night." Lucy's red hair was long, wavy and thick.

She had blue eyes and a freckled face. Very Irish-looking. Her jeans were Calvin Klein's and the logo on her T-shirt said, "Save the Redwoods." Neither girl was as petite as Lisa, but they weren't by any means big women.

"Hi," they both said in unison.

"Hello, ladies."

Even though I frequently called Jean "girl," just as she called me "boy," I wasn't going to make that mistake with any or all of these three. No doubt they wouldn't appreciate it like Jean.

"Lisa tells me you know Karen. Do you have any idea where she might be? Have you seen her or spoken to her recently?"

"No, not recently. I think it was like last quarter." Diana was the first to speak.

Lucy chimed in, "I saw her once in summer. Maybe like July. Downtown. Like I saw her through the open front door of Camouflage. She saw me, so I went in and talked to her. She was like looking at a very sexy bra and panties. Yuh know, like black lace and real skimpy? Almost a thong."

"How'd she seem? Yuh know, her emotional state. Did she seem nervous or out of sorts in any way?"

"Not really. Seemed more embarrassed than anything. Like she was all embarrassed that I caught her in that store. Other than that, no. She didn't seem like scared or anything like that."

That store had some fairly lurid window displays, racy lingerie, sexy bras and panties on mannequins that were posed suggestively. They had a back room with sex toys and pornographic literature. One time they had Candida Royalle as a guest speaker talking about her recently created production company, Femme Productions, whose goal is to make adult films based on female desire, and couples therapy.

"And you, Lisa? When was the last time you saw her or talked to her?"

"End of last quarter."

"Can any of you ladies tell me who her adviser is, or any of the other teachers she's particularly close to?"

"Oh, yeah," Lisa said. "Her official adviser is like Dr. Stein. Dr. Dov Stein, sociology professor. But I think she gets more advice, both academic and personal, from like Darryl Routh." She pronounced it Ruth. "Dr. Stein's like all uptight, but she actually seems to like it that way. A good example is he insists on being called 'doctor,' and don't ever call him 'doc.' Karen's a real traditionalist. She likes calling him Dr. Stein. She wishes all her professors would do it that way, but they don't. Almost all the other ones go by their first names, and she struggles with that. Darryl likes to go by his first name, but Karen likes to call him Mr. Routh. He was a lecturer. I say 'was' because he didn't like have tenure, so he was like done at the end of spring quarter. A.B.D. in the doctoral program in sociology."

"A.B.D.? Think I know what that is."

"Stands for 'all but dissertation.' Yuh know, like he did everything except write his thesis, so he got like an M.A. and a year contract as a lecturer. Him and Karen are all like very close. Her and Dr. Stein are close, too, but I think she's closer to Darryl. Seems like she talks to him more'n she talks to Dr. Stein, which is like weird because Darryl always refers to Dr. Stein as 'doc,' and Karen always like scolds him when he does it."

"She a good student?"

"Oh, the best! Her evaluations have always been excellent, and when she got a letter grade, it was always like an A. Yuh know we got to pick our own adviser when we like went into sophomore year, and she chose Dr. Stein. I think she did it *because* she was such a good student and he was so strict. She liked the discipline and the challenge."

"How can I get in touch with these two gentlemen?"

"I don't like know what Darryl's phone number is, but I do know he rents a room in the Palomar Inn. He's like one of the reasons Karen got a room there. She could've like gotten a room in the row house next door, but like she wanted to move into the Palomar. Darryl like hangs out at the bar that's in the Cooper House, and when there's a band playing, he'll be out on the front patio. Dr. Stein's got an office at College Eight. You could like call up there and find out his office hours. I'm sure he'll be there tomorrow."

"You know where Darryl's from?"

"Like New York, I think, but I'm not sure."

I wrote it down in my notebook.

"Anything else about them that might help my investigation?"

"I heard Darryl like all bragging once that he was in prison, but I don't know if it's like true or he was just trying to impress somebody. It sure didn't impress me. I think the guy's like kind a' creepy. I don't know what Karen sees in him."

"How 'bout Jason?" I asked, referring to Danielle's list. "I don't know his last name, and I don't have a phone number on him. Think he knows anything?"

"Last name's Jordon. Two ohs. I got his phone number."

She took off upstairs and came back with an address book. She found his number, and I wrote it down next to his name on Danielle's list.

"He might know something. They used to like study together a lot. He's like still taking classes. I'm in one with him. Graduates in June like the rest of us. Lives down on Lighthouse Avenue off West Cliff. I been there once. Little old garage that they made into a cottage. It's like around Santa Cruz Street and Monterey Street. In that neighborhood. It's just one block from the beach he likes to surf at."

"And Rebecca Ginsberg? Know her? Think she might know anything?"

"Rebecca graduated last June, but so far she's stayed in town. She's been living at the Palomar the last couple years. She's like from New York. Rich girl. Parents both passed away. I heard she's like got a trust fund. Has a regular monthly income."

"She know Darryl?"

"She's all like real good friends with him."

"Think they might've known each other in New York?"

"Maybe. I don't like know for sure."

"When's the last time you saw her?"

"Gee, I think it was at the end of spring quarter. Don't know her as good as I like know Karen. If I was as friendly with her as I am with Karen, I wouldn't worry about her like I'm worried about Karen. I would say that Rebecca's not at all vulnerable. She can take care of herself. She's all like a tough girl. I don't mean tough like a biker chick; I mean tough like no-nonsense. She uses her sex to get what she wants. I wouldn't ever like mess with her myself."

The other two women were silent throughout this exchange. It was obvious they didn't know Karen as well as Lisa did. They probably didn't know Rebecca at all. Their eyes were glazing over. I could see they were eager to get back to their studies, or more aptly, they wanted to get the hell out of there, get up to Cafezinho at the north end of the Mall in the courtyard behind Bookshop. Or maybe even go next door to Lulu Carpenter's for an ice-cold beer. Whatever else they wanted to do, they damn sure didn't want to hang around and answer any more of my questions.

"All right, ladies. You've all been a great help. Thank you."

And with that I headed out the door.

Four

Back at the house, Jean's message was on my answering machine. She picked up when I returned her call.

"Hi, Doll. Thanks for getting back to me. Sorry I wasn't here to answer the phone. I just picked up a new case this afternoon and was out on my first lead when you called."

"So, I guess you want something from me? Let's see now. How long's it been since we went out to lunch at El Palomar?"

"Aw, come on. I just been really busy. Hey, let's set up a date right now."

"Not go'n'a be that easy, fella'."

I knew when she called me "fella'" that she wasn't nearly as bummed as she pretended to be, but I went along with her little charade.

"Okay. Wha'da yuh want me to do?" I said putting on my best guilty inflection. "I'm so sorry."

"Gotcha, didn't I?"

"You're just kiddin'?" All innocence. I acted like I didn't know what she was up to. "Aw, you were really making me feel guilty there." It was hard to mask my sarcasm. "You wouldn't't've gotten away with it if I's lookin' you in the eye, and you know it."

"So, what can I do for you this time?"

I gave her a quick outline of the case and started out with the first two names.

"Probably a good thing I was out when you called. Gave me time to get more info. Got a name from the interview I was at. Didn't have it before. Can you check out a guy named Darryl Routh?" I gave her the right pronunciation and then spelled it out. "Think he's from New York. Came here as a grad. student at the U. but didn't finish the program. Worked a year as a lecturer on campus. Might have a record. One of the women I just spoke to told me he bragged about doing time. She didn't know if it was true or if it was some kind of a false boast. Also, could you check out my missing person? Karen Babbit. Supposed to be starting her senior year. Here we are a month into the fall quarter, and she hasn't been to any of her classes. Not answering her phone or returning calls either."

"Anything else?" she said with a fake show of sarcasm.

I would've liked for her to run Dr. Dov Stein and Rebecca Ginsberg, too, but that would've been pushing it with the two names I'd already given her. She'd be in trouble enough with her lieutenant for getting the information I'd already asked her for.

"Yeah. Let's get together for lunch. How 'bout tomorrow? Noon at El Palomar?"

"See yuh there. Maybe I'll have something for you. 'Bye, big fella'."

When she did these favors for me, we kept

things on the up-and-up. We always did Dutch treat whenever we went out. We didn't want even the appearance of impropriety.

I got the phone book out and looked up the number of Stein's office on campus. I couldn't find his office number, but there was a listing for the sociology department. I wrote it down next to his name in my notebook and dialed it. A woman informed me in a pleasant voice that he'd be in his office the next day Friday at eleven. I'd try to be there by a quarter to.

One more thing to do on the case before going surfing. Try Karen's phone number. I probably should've done that first, but things just started rolling, and before I knew it, I was talking to those women and Jean. I dialed the number and got a recorded message that said it was disconnected. I hung up and called Danielle.

"When was the last time you tried to reach Karen by phone?" I asked.

"Monday like I said. Why?"

"'Cause I just tried the number you gave me, and it's been disconnected."

"Really?"

"Yes, indeed."

She told me to hold for a minute, and when she came back on the line, she read off the number I had written down, so I told her I'd check into it and talk to her later. That was about as far as I could go for that day. Time to go surfing.

I got my bike and Wheele out of the garage. After I hooked it all up and leaned it against the back-yard fence, I got my board down off the racks on the wall above where the bike and Wheele were stored. I took the board into the back yard, put it down on the lawn, and waxed it. Then I got into my wetsuit and booties. Next was sunscreen, and it went everywhere on my face and neck, but not my forehead. I had a pink baseball cap that covered everything from my eyebrows up. It had an O'Neill Cold Water Classic surf contest insignia in front. I put the board on the Wheele and headed down to Cowell's, where I locked it up to one of the railings in front of the Dream Inn. I paddled out to the lineup and waited for my first wave.

There weren't many guys out, a few in the lineup and a few more paddling back out from riding a wave. School was just letting out about then, so I expected this lineup to get crowded soon. There was one guy who was a few feet to the right of a cluster of guys who all seemed to know each other. He was about my age with graying dark hair and beard. He wore tinted swim goggles. I figured they were prescription lenses. It's hard to catch a wave if you can't see the damn thing. We nodded at each other. I got into a spot between him and the group to the left. As we sat on our boards waiting for a wave, a younger guy with long brown hair paddled out toward us. He was the same guy who was riding a wave in as I was paddling out.

"Wow, Dr. Stein!" he said. "What a great ride that was!"

"Yes indeed. Maybe now I'll get one."

I was completely taken aback. Here was one, maybe two of the people I wanted to talk to about Karen. What're the chances? I decided not to say anything to either of them out here, not even know-ing for sure if the younger one was Jason Jordon. I'd find out soon enough that he was indeed Jordon. As for the other guy, I'd take a ride up to campus the next day and call on him in his office.

The best part of that trip was going to be the ride home, which had one of the best views of Mon-terey Bay in the entire county. In fact, right at that moment, we could see some of the buildings on campus from right there in the water at Cowell's. I really was living in paradise and this was the best season. Indian summer. It was about eighty degrees that day and the skies were clear. The after-school crowd was starting to trickle down the stairs with their boards. It was about to get really crowded.

I stayed in the water for over two hours. At low tide there were at least fifty surfers out, but I got plenty of rides. Most of them were party waves. That's a wave that you're riding with at least one other person, but usually it's more like three, four or five people. Nobody I knew was out that day, so all the party waves I caught were with strangers. For-tunately, none of those people were "agro," as the saying goes, but that's the kind of break Cowell's is, strictly for old men, little kids and beginners. Jesse, one of the regulars, calls it Cowellskiki. That's what kind of a small, long break it is. The kind of break that Brian Wilson must have had in mind when he wrote, "Catch a wave/And you're sittin' on top of the world." When I got out, I had a grin on my face, and I was feeling just fine.

I went home, took a shower and went over to China Szechuan for some Kung Pao Chicken and

Mu-chu Pork with four pancakes. Then I took a walk up the Mall to the Palomar Inn. The directory showed that the office was on the mezzanine level of the building. That was all I needed right then. I planned to go up there the next day after lunch and talk to whoever was at the desk. Back on the street, I headed up to the north end of Pacific to Lulu Carpenter's and had a beer. Then I went home and worked up my schedule for Friday. I'm one of those early-to-bed-early-to-rise kind of guys. By the time I finished with my schedule, it was nine o'clock, so I made one more call before going to bed. It was Jason Jordon's number. His answering machine picked up, so I left him my name and number, and then got ready to hit the sack.

Five

The next morning, I was up by five-thirty as usual. Mornings in late spring and early summer when there are good low tides and a sandbar, I try to surf dawn patrol as often as I can. But this was mid-October, the start of the winter season when the minus tides and the swells were kicking up later in the day. The first thing I did that morning was my routine of two hundred sit-ups. Then I fixed my usual breakfast for Friday, cold high-fiber cereal with chocolate hemp milk, an Eggo blueberry waffle and orange juice to wash down all the vitamin and mineral supplements I liked to take. After breakfast I went out to my back patio where there was an outdoor shower with hot and cold water.

After my shower I hopped on my bike and rode out to West Cliff Drive. I got off the bike path at Gharkey Street and peddled over to Lighthouse Avenue. Just past Santa Cruz Street on the right was a small, old two-car garage that looked like it'd been converted into a living space. It fit the description of Jason's place that Lisa had told me about yesterday. A sheet metal smokestack punched through the roof. The garage doors were still at-

Jerome Arthur

tached, but you could see that they were sealed off.
This had to be where Jason Jordon lived.

I peddled past it to Monterey Street, back to
the bike path and out to Natural Bridges. I didn't
take any more detours on the ride. Low tide was
long past (not very low to begin with) so there
weren't any surfers in the water at Cowell's. Steam-
er Lane out at the point, which I thought was one of
the best, if not *the* best, point breaks in California,
was a better break at medium tide. There were a few
guys out at the Lane. When I got back into downtown, I peddled up the Mall, over to Center Street
and back to my cottage. Cool ride, a lot like a good
surfing session. It was like yesterday when I got out
of the water. I was feeling good.

It was nine o'clock, about an hour and a half
before I'd leave for campus, so I went into my office and finished the insurance company report I
was working on yesterday and walked it up to the
post office and mailed it. The line was long, so by
the time I got back home, it was ten o'clock.

There was one other thing I wanted to do before going up to see Stein. Lil had some clients who
were U.C. professors, so I popped in on her to see if
she knew him. When I opened her front door, the
shop was unoccupied, and she came out the door
that went into her bedroom.

"Hey, Lil. What's up?"

"Not much, Jack. What're you up to?"

"I was just on my way up to campus to interview one of the professors whose name came up
in a case I'm working. You recognize the name Dr.
Dov Stein?"

35

"Yup. He's one of my clients. Been cutting his hair and trimming his beard for maybe five years. Got a standing appointment."

"Anything you can tell me about him that might help me? Don't want yuh to violate your barber/client confidentiality or anything."

She laughed at that.

"Don't know much. Guy's a real egghead. Real quiet. Told me right away he likes to be called 'Dr. Stein.' I call 'im by his first name, and he said it was okay. Keeps coming back, so he must not mind too much. He said just don't call him 'doc.' Likes looking at my *Playboy* magazines. I think his field is sociology. Doesn't talk much. Wears a wedding ring so he must be married. What's your case?"

"Missing person. He's the adviser of the coed I'm lookin' for. Go'n'a see if he knows anything.

A client came in her front door just as I finished that thought.

"Hey, John. How yuh doin'?"

"'Mornin', Lil. What's up?"

"Okay, Lil. Thanks," I said and headed out the door.

I got in the car and drove up to campus. It had been a long time since I'd been up there. In the interest of professional advancement, I took some Legal Studies classes there in 1980 after I got my certificate in Administration of Justice at Cabrillo. That came after ten years' work as a checker at Safeway. Four years before Safeway I was an undergrad. at San José State majoring in Spanish. I thought I wanted to be a teacher once, but when the time came to go for my credential, there weren't any jobs, and I was burned out on going to school. So, when I graduated, I joined the retail clerk's union and went to work at Safeway. It was when I got burned out doing that that I decided to be a detective.

Stein's office was at College Eight. The parking was tight, but there was a metered visitor spot a short distance from the buildings. It was a quarter to eleven when I got to his office. The door was closed and locked, so I waited, browsing the notices posted on a corkboard on the wall between his office and the next one down the hall. Eight and a half by eleven colored sheets were thumb tacked to the cork, advertising six-week courses abroad, mostly foreign language courses in French, German and Spanish. Boy, was this ever taking me back.

At about five to eleven, the guy I'd seen in the water on Thursday came down the hall, a cute young coed by his side. This time he was dressed a little more professorially. The swim goggles were replaced with wire-rim glasses. Instead of the wet-suit, he wore a white shirt, tie and a tweed jacket with leather patches on the elbows. All of this was topped off by a brown fur-felt fedora with a black ribbon a good inch and a half wide. He wasn't exactly dressed for Indian Summer, although his tweed jacket did look light weight.

"Dr. Stein?" I said when he got close enough.

"Yes?"

He passed me and continued on to his office

door. I followed.

"My name's Jack Lefevre, and I'd like to talk to you about Karen Babbit. She seems to be missing, and I was hired to find her."

"Oh, yes," he said unlocking his door. "One moment please."

I followed him and the girl into the office where he rifled through some papers on his desktop and handed one of them to her.

"Thank you, Dr. Stein," she said and left.

His office looked to me like all the college professor's offices I'd ever seen at the three colleges I'd gone to. Papers all over his desktop, and books stacked randomly in bookcases along two of the four walls.

"You look familiar," he said. "Have we met?"

"We haven't actually met. I was out at Cowell's yesterday at low tide."

"That's right. How may I be of assistance?" he asked.

At least he was acting concerned. I wasn't quite sure if it was an act or the real thing.

"For starters, when did you last see Karen?"

"At the end of the spring quarter. That's when she told me she was going to be in my Social Problems class this quarter. She hasn't been to class since the quarter started, and now I just picked this up from my mailbox in the office."

He handed me a withdrawal slip. That's when I noticed his wedding ring. Stein's class title was printed in block letters at the top. Karen's name was hand-printed on one line and her signature on a line underneath it.

"Does this look like her handwriting and signature?"

"Yes, it does."

At least now I knew she was just missing, not dead.

"So, she must've been here on campus sometime. When?"

"Well," he said, stretching the syllable out. "I picked up my mail yesterday at about noon. The admissions office closes at five. So, I'd say she was probably on campus sometime during those hours. She might have dropped it off this morning. Or maybe somebody dropped it off for her. Today is the last day to withdraw without penalty."

"What was she studying in your class this quarter?"

"Why would you want to know that?"

"If I know what she's interested in, what she's studying, I'll get a clearer picture of who she is."

"I see. If you think it will help, I will try. The class is really only a survey, and since she hasn't been to any of the sessions, I'm not sure what she was going to focus on, but the last couple of quarters she has shown strong interest in social conditions in the barrio. She has been spending quite a bit of time down in Beach Flats. You were aware that she has Latino heritage through her mother, weren't you?"

I had to admit I didn't know that. That'd be something I'd have to talk to Danielle about. It would've been nice if she'd shared that little nugget of information with me. Was that all she wasn't telling me? Of course, I should have figured it out on my own. Danielle looked like she might have some Hispanic heritage. And the picture of Karen she gave me should have been a clue. Except for the blue eyes, she had the same dark hair and olive complexion, though lighter, as Danielle.

"Do you have any idea where she might be?" I asked.

"Not a clue. I'm just as surprised by her disappearance as anybody. And I'll tell you, I can't be more disappointed. She's one of the best students I've ever had, both in the classroom and when I've acted as her adviser. Really smart. Likes the subject matter. Thrives on the discipline. One of the few students to call me by my title, which I prefer, without resentment. I just can't imagine where she could have gone. I view this as very irresponsible behavior. Completely unlike her."

"I understand that she's close to a former faculty member, Darryl Routh? Know anything about that?"

"First of all, let me say, he never was a faculty member on this staff. Yes, I know him. And now that he is no longer a lecturer here, I don't think I'd be violating any code of ethics by telling you that I don't consider him to be a reputable person. I wouldn't be surprised if he knew exactly where Miss Babbit is, and I don't believe that his intentions are honorable and/or altruistic."

"Why do you say that?"

"He's a slick operator, that one. If Karen were my daughter, I would forbid her associating with him. As it is, she spends far too much time consulting with him on academic matters."

"Doesn't sound like you have a very high opinion of him? You have anything other than opinion?"

"I don't have any concrete evidence to support what I think. And I don't want to be a source of gossip, so I'll just keep my suspicions to myself."

"How about Jason Jordon? You know him?"

"He was that young man who was in the water yesterday. Lives just around the corner from where we were surfing."

"Was that the young fellow who was sticking close to you?"

"'Sticking.' That does describe it, doesn't it?"

"You kind of wish he'd buzz off?"

"Oh, I wouldn't put it that way. He's a nice enough young fellow. He thinks it's enough just to associate with intellectuals and be gracious. He doesn't have the kind of restraint that Miss Babbit possesses. I'm exceedingly amenable to her attraction to traditions and customs. He's a little more innovative shall we say."

This guy was killing me with his vocabulary. I'd forgotten what it was like to be in college.

"How about Rebecca Ginsberg? She ever take any of your classes?"

"Once again, I have to ask, what does it have to do with Miss Babbit?"

"And once again, I have to answer, maybe nothing, maybe everything. You are aware that Rebecca and Karen are good friends? And it seems

Rebecca might be missing, too. At least no one's seen her for a while. So, if you know anything that would help me to locate these two women, I'd appreciate it if you'd tell me."

"Miss Ginsberg was in my Social Problems class in the spring quarter. That's the same course Miss Babbit was supposed to be taking this quarter. She was examining prostitution as a social construct and its impact on the communities where it is practiced. She has been spending time in River Flats. You know, the neighborhood around Ocean and Barson? A lot of prostitution present in that neighborhood."

"So, if I'm lucky, I might find either or both of the young women down in those neighborhoods?"

"You might."

And that was just about all I could get out of the good professor. I had this gnawing feeling there was something he wasn't telling me. Just as I thought Danielle wasn't telling me everything, I was sure Stein was also hiding something, but he seemed much more devious about it. Whereas Danielle was probably holding out because she thought she knew something bad about Karen, Stein was holding back because he didn't want to reveal some dark secret about himself. At least that's the way I read it.

I thanked Stein, gave him my card, told him to call me if he thought of anything else, and headed back to my car. It was getting on to 11:45, so I hustled down the hill and made it to El Palomar in time to meet Jean.

Six

It was five after twelve when Jean and I met in front of El Palomar. She's a tall girl, about five-eleven, and in her high heels a good three inches taller than I. She's hard to miss with her dark hair and blue eyes, a striking beauty. We walked through the hotel lobby to the restaurant.

"I came by here late yesterday," I said as we passed the elevator and the stairs up to the rooms. "Go'n'a go upstairs after lunch, see if I can find out anything about Karen Babbit."

"Probably won't have much luck with that. She moved out Monday. One of the things I found out in my search."

"Yeah, I actually found that out yesterday myself when I tried to call her number. Disconnected. She's also dropped her classes, or at least one of them, this quarter. Did that yesterday. So, she's not exactly missing now. More like she's unseen. You get a forwarding address?"

"Nope. But you might check with the office upstairs here, anyway."

"I was go'n'a do that soon's we finish our lunch."

Oh, Hard Tuesday

We were seated in a booth. We ordered lunch specials, she the chile relleno, and I the snapper. As we waited for our lunches, Jean took a notebook out of her purse.

"As I said before, your missing person, Karen Babbit, has moved out of the Palomar," she said, looking at the notebook. "Couldn't find anything else on her. Record seems to be clean.

"Now, this Darryl Routh is a different story. He's got a sheet. Mostly small stuff. Had a pot bust when he was in college. Columbia. New York City where he grew up. Also had a joyriding bust in high school. Seems he took his dad's car without permission. Father was the one who filed the complaint. I'm guessing the kid was a problem from the get-go. Old man finally got fed up. Just the fact they had a car in New York City tells you something about how affluent the family of this kid is.

"Worked his way up the crime ladder when he was in college. Most serious bust was brandishing a firearm. Pulled a Derringer on another student at a fraternity party. Gun was registered, so he basically got off with a slap on the wrist and was sent home. Dad probably pulled some strings to get 'im off. I'm just guessing, but I think he's got a romanticized self-image, hence the Derringer, and plenty of money to pull it off. This next thing really caught my eye. Got busted for pandering three years ago."

She slid a mug shot across the table to me. What I saw was the picture of a preppy-looking kid with a cocky smirk. He had a longish Ivy League hairstyle, a bright, entitled look in his eyes, and a ruddy complexion. His perfect nose and ears showed his patrician heritage.

"Charges dropped. Insufficient evidence. Came to Santa Cruz shortly after that. Been a grad. student and lecturer up at the U. ever since, but now he's finished there, too."

"Really. One of the other people I talked to, Dov Stein, a prof., doesn't have much use for him. Now I understand why. Just talked to 'im about an hour ago. That's how I found out about Karen dropping her classes. I think this Routh character tries to give people the impression he was a professor, but he was only a lecturer. Stein got offended when I referred to Routh as a faculty member."

"Think you can trust what Stein says?"

"Don't think he's telling me everything; nor do I think my client's telling me everything. Although, motivations are different."

"Hmm."

"How'd yuh get this mug shot past Jenkins?"

"Wasn't easy, but I managed it. Copied it when he was on his break."

"Cocky lookin' little snot, isn't he?"

"Doesn't look like the kind a' person I'd wan'a know."

"Looks like my work's cut out for me. As much as he was denying it, I think this guy Stein knows more about Routh, and Karen for that matter, than he's letting on. 'Fact, I think he might even be closer to Routh than he wants anybody to believe. I'd sure like to have a chat with 'im, but then if he's anything like Stein, I'm probably not go'n'a learn any more'n I already know. I just hope he's not as scarce as Karen and Rebecca, although Karen was just on campus yesterday dropping her classes. The other two seem to be missing in action here. I hope they're not a 'threesome' if you know what I mean."

"I know *exactly* what you mean," she said with a knowing look in her beautiful blue eyes.

We finished our lunches, paid the bill and headed out of the restaurant. We hugged and said our goodbyes. Jean went back to work as I went up the stairs to the office of the Palomar Inn. Sitting behind the desk in a dingy little office was a skinny, derelict looking little guy with mousy features who came across as someone who smoked one too many cigarettes and drank one too many shots of cheap bourbon. He looked up as I approached.

"There's a minimum three month wait for rooms here," he said before I could state my business. "Longer if you want low income."

"Hold on there," I said, by way of cutting him off. "I'm not looking for a room; I want some information about one of your tenants. Actually, she's a former tenant, and I was wondering if she left a forwarding address. Name's Karen Babbit. Know who I'm talking about?"

"Yep."

I could see that this was going to be like pulling teeth.

"Yep, you know who I'm talking about, or yep, she left a forwarding address?"

"Oh, I know who you're talking about all right. Just moved out on Monday and didn't leave a forwarding address."

"How 'bout a couple of others? Rebecca

Ginsberg and Darryl Routh."

"Yuh know, I think I already told you too much about Karen Babbit. People live here expect a certain amount of privacy."

I took a twenty out of my wallet and put it on the desk in front of him. The money was gone so quickly that I thought the little scrounge might have been a magician. Now you see it; now you don't.

"I know you know that at least one, maybe both of those women moved out, so since they're not your tenants anymore, I think you can be a little more forthcoming with any information you might have on them. Now it seems both women are missing."

"Don't know much. They were real good friends. Moved in about the same time; moved out together. I overheard 'em talkin'. Sounded like they got 'em a split-level apartment together out in Live Oak someplace. Seventeenth, Chanticleer, one a' them Live Oak streets. Seemed you couldn't separate 'em. Nobody could."

"How 'bout Routh? He still live here?"

"'Nother Jackson'd jog my memory."

I slipped him another twenty.

"Yeah, he still lives here."

"Don't suppose you could tell me his room number?"

"Could, but it'd take a little more to sweeten the pot."

I pulled out another ten. I figured fifty bucks was plenty enough.

"Four-twenty. Got a view a' the Mall. Don't know if he's in right now, but you could go up and check."

The stairs were right next to the office door, so I headed up. I'm one of these guys who doesn't use elevators. I figure I will when I have to, but in the meantime, I get a good workout when I use the stairs, so that's the way I go. When I got to the fourth floor, I was fairly winded. I'd taken the stairs two at a time.

I knocked on the door and got no answer. I tried again. Still nothing. I got my lock picks out and was inside in less than a minute. The room was a complete mess. I saw an open newspaper on the nightstand next to the telephone. It was the local daily, dated yesterday, open to the want ads. One column was handyman services, another massage. The beginning of the apartments-for-rent column was on the right side of the page. I quickly skimmed handyman and didn't see anything that remotely resembled a lead. The massage column was a different story. I only had to read three of the ads before I realized that this was just a place for call girls to advertise. There were ads for outcall and incall massage. There was only one that advertised "therapeutic massage."

I set the paper down and looked around. Typical bachelor pad. Dishes were piled up in the sink, the bed was unmade, and not all the clothes were put away. In contrast to this scene, there was some pretty expensive looking photo and video equipment stored neatly in one corner of the room. I went over and gave it a closer look and could see that it was professional equipment. I gave the rest of the place a quick scan, didn't see anything particularly noteworthy, and left.

I was planning on going surfing again, and it was still a couple hours before low tide, so I decided to take another bike ride out to Lighthouse Avenue, see if I could have a chat with Jason Jordon. I was hoping he'd give me a lead of some kind. So far, the only people I'd spoken to were the three coeds, whom I believed, and the college professor, whom I didn't believe completely. I don't know what it was. Call it a hunch, a gut feeling, whatever. I just wasn't buying everything he was selling. I hadn't even met this guy Darryl Routh yet, but I'd already heard enough about him to know not to trust anything he might say.

Seven

I arrived at Jason's cottage at about two o'clock. The same guy I'd seen yesterday in the water with Stein came through the front door as I approached. He looked slightly different in jeans and T-shirt than he did in a wetsuit on a surfboard. That was normal. His long brown hair, longer than was the style at the time, wasn't quite as dark as it had been when it was wet. In fact, it had a trace of sun-bleached blond running through it. He was taller than I thought yesterday, about my height, but his tanned good looks hadn't changed since then.

He looked at me, nodded, and in a friendly tone, said,

"'T's up?"

"You Jason?

"Uh, huh. Who're you, and wha'da yuh want?"

His tone changed slightly. It hadn't become unpleasant, but it wasn't all that friendly, either. He struck me as an earnest young man, a real Jimmy Olsen type. He was holding a brand new, still-in-the-plastic-wrapping, surfboard leash in one hand and a cake of Sex Wax in the other.

"My name's Jack Lefevre. You get the voicemail message I left last night?"

"Oh, yeah. What'd yuh want?"

"Wanted to talk to you 'bout Karen Babbit."

"Yeah?" He was wary.

"So, you know she's missing."

"Yeah, I *do* know." The look of concern seemed genuine. His tone was shifting back to pleasant.

"You know anything that might help me find her? Her family's concerned. They haven't spoken to or heard from her for quite some time now."

"I've been really worried about her, too. Haven't seen her since the end of spring quarter. Don't think she's been to any of her classes this term. Last time I went by her place at the Palomar, she was gone, moved out. Rebecca, too. You know Rebecca?"

"We haven't met, but I've heard about her since I started looking for Karen. Think she might know something about Karen's disappearance?"

"Might. Karen sure does pay attention to what Rebecca says. Rebecca's more worldly'n Karen. Parents're both gone. Been on her own since she was fifteen?"

"I heard that."

"Yeah, she just seems so much more savvy than other girls her age. Definitely more than Karen or Lisa. You know Lisa?"

"We've met."

I wasn't saying much here because Jason seemed to want to talk, and I wanted to let him. He might've known something that he didn't think he

51

knew, and with a little bit of luck I might hear him blurt it out.

"Tell me more about Rebecca."

"She's just so much more sophisticated than most a' the girls her age, 'least most a' the girls her age I know. Dresses real sexy and uses it to try to get stuff. Seems more like twenty-five 'r thirty than twenty-two. I heard she was approached by Hefner to do the centerfold in *Playboy* before she came to Santa Cruz. Claims he didn't take her 'cause she was only seventeen at the time."

"So that was when? Five years ago?"

"About. I think she was still a senior in high school."

"You know where that was?"

"New York. Some girls's prep school in Manhattan. Never mentioned the name. Don't know where she got the idea to come out here. Think she did it mostly to get away from her uncle. He's the one takes care of her trust fund."

"She ever mention his name?"

"Uncle Chris is all she ever said. Don't know if it's her dad's brother or who. Last name could be Ginsberg."

"That first name spelled the usual way, C-H-R-I-S?"

"I think so."

I wrote it down in my notebook along with the other information he'd given me. The thought occurred to me that he might spell it K-R-I-S. After all, the last name sounded German to me. Thankfully, that first name, however it was spelled, would make it easier to find Ginsberg in the New York phone book, easier than if it were say, Abe or Ari. I was quite sure that there were a lot of Ginsbergs in Manhattan, so it was going to be plenty hard to find anybody with that name on that island, no matter what the first name.

"So, you know anything else that might shed some light on Karen's whereabouts?"

"Not really. First time since I've known her that she's done something like this."

"You know Darryl Routh?"

His face darkened.

"Yeah, I know 'im." He almost spat the words out. "Don't like 'im. Don't know what it is makes Karen like 'im, but she does. Rebecca, too. She's more his speed. Both from New York. I think they might've known each other there. Don't know that for sure, but they act like they've known each other a long time. Know how you can tell? Smooth, too smooth for me."

"You seen either one of those two lately?"

"Rebecca, no, but I did see Routh last week. He was hanging out on the patio in front of the Cooper House listening to the band. You know, Warmth? Routh was there with another guy, bigger'n you and me. They were just having drinks. Didn't look like they were eating."

"And the women weren't anywhere around?"

"Didn't see 'em. I heard he hangs out there quite a bit. He'll prob'ly be there for sure this afternoon. Friday's a big day at that restaurant. 'Specially when there's live music. He won't miss it. Me, I'd rather go surfing."

"And how about Dov Stein? How tight are he and Routh?"

"Not tight at all. 'Fact I don't think Dr. Stein likes 'im much either, and I'm sure the feelings're mutual. 'Least that's how it looks."

"All right, Jason. You've been a big help here. Thanks. You might be hearing from me again. You headin' to Cowell's? Catch some waves?"

"Yup," he said as he started to move toward the back of his cottage.

Leaning up against the back wall was a nice eight-two Johnny Rice mini longboard.

"Nice board," I said. "You know Johnny? He surfs Cowell's all the time."

"Don't know 'im, but I've seen him in the water."

"Maybe I'll see yuh out there. Thinking about goin' out myself."

I went out to where my bike was locked up to the stop sign at the corner and peddled back into downtown. The first place I went was the library to look for Chris Ginsberg's address and phone number in the New York phone book. I found two Chris Ginsbergs, three Carls and five C. Ginsbergs. No Krises or K.s. I copied down the numbers and addresses of all the Chrises and C.s in my notebook and headed over to the Oak Room at the Cooper House.

I always thought Don Henley's song "Sunset Grill" was a good description of the Cooper House. Which was unfortunate, because the building was originally a beautiful old courthouse. It was built in the 1890s, a brick and stone beauty with turrets, cupolas and dormers. Crenulations decorated the roof-line beneath the rain gutters. In the early seventies, an enterprising and creative developer named Max Walden bought and restored the structure. He named the building the Cooper House and the anchor businesses on the ground floor were the Wild Thyme Restaurant and the Oak Room bar with the enclosed patio in front. Other retail businesses— leather, jewelry and apparel boutiques—occupied the rear and Cooper Street side of the building, and the upper floors.

Almost immediately after the restaurant opened in 1972, Max brought in Don McCaslin's band Warmth to play the outdoor patio. This turned out to be a huge success. Ginger, an older woman (probably in her eighties) who lived downtown, appeared as the Rainbow Lady on the patio and side-walk. She wore big, flowing ankle-length dresses and matching floppy hats that sported every color in the rainbow as she shook and heeled her tambourine and danced to the music. This party atmosphere prevailed for some time after Max sold the building, but the new owner was definitely changing things.

Don's band was already playing when I got there. A good crowd occupied most of the tables. It was a little before three o'clock. We were still on daylight savings time, and would be till the end of the month, so we'd have another three hours of daylight. The band usually packed up a little before twilight time.

I saw Routh right away. He was sitting at the tables along the side under the windows of the bar. That was the spot usually reserved for friends of the band. Routh was wearing chinos, a short sleeve aloha shirt and a pair of Wayfarers. His hair was combed better here than it was in the mug shot. The smirk on his preppy face was ubiquitous. Sitting next to him behind the table on the left was a black man wearing a cowboy hat. On the other side, in the closest seat to the band at Routh's table, was a big blond guy who had a pasty barroom complexion. He was wearing Ray Bans and was dressed pretty flamboyantly in a big-collar white shirt, a royal blue sport jacket with wide lapels, and white slacks, belt and shoes. I'm five-eleven and in good shape, mostly I think because I surf and ride a bike, and I can handle myself in a street fight. It was hard to tell because he was sitting down, but it looked like Pasty Face had me by a couple inches and maybe twenty pounds. I was sizing him up in case he turned out to be Routh's muscle and I'd have to defend myself against him. It was obvious that Routh wasn't his own muscle. He looked scrawny next to Pasty Face.

They both had bottles of beer sitting on the table in front of them. The black guy was a regular there when the band was playing, and he didn't look like he was hanging with Preppy Boy and Pasty Face. They were both smoking, and you could see that he was wishing they'd go somewhere else.

One of Don's regular singers, a guy I knew named David Barnes, who sounded a lot like Frank Sinatra, was singing "Wee Small Hours of the Morning" into the mic. When he saw me, he gave me the high sign, so I decided to wait till he took a break and talk to him. The break came when he finished the song.

"You know the guy sitting next to the black cowboy?" I asked when David got over to where I was standing. Routh and Pasty Face hadn't moved. The black cowboy got up and went over to talk to the guy on congas.

"You mean the preppy in the Hawaiian shirt? Not really. He's been hangin' around for a while now. 'Course, yuh know I'm only here on weekends, so I don't really know everybody. Why? What's up?"

"How 'bout his buddy with the barroom tan? They always together?"

"Most of the time. Why yuh askin'?"

"I'm looking for a missing person, and he might know something about it."

"Really?"

"Maybe, maybe not. But I'm pretty sure he does know something. Think he'll be here tomorrow?"

"Probably. He was here last Friday and Saturday and the weekend before that, too."

"Cool. What time you guys go'n'a be startin' tomorrow?"

"Band starts playin' around noon. I got'a work at the gas station mini mart till noon. Prob'ly get here a little before one."

"Okay, I'm go'n'a try to be here around that time. I wan'a talk to 'im. He always sit on the side like that?"

"Every time I've seen 'im."

"He know anybody in the band?"

"Don't think so. Just kind a' started sittin'

there. I think the big guy pushes his weight around."

That was all David knew, and the other players were starting to pick up their instruments, so he went back over to the bandstand. I really wanted to catch some waves before the day ended, so I peddled back to my bungalow. Before I got my board out, I peeked in on Lil. She was cutting a guy's hair.

"Hey, Lil. How'd you like to go out to dinner tonight? I'll treat."

"Where yuh wan'a go?"

"I was thinkin' Italian. Santa Cruz Hotel. Go next door afterwards. Drinks in the Red Room."

"It's a date. What time?"

"I'm goin' surfin' right now, but I should be back home by five-thirty, six o'clock. Wha'da yuh say we make it seven."

"Great! I'll be ready by seven. See yuh then."

I went out to Cowell's. Caught some waves. It was a good day. Jason was out, and so was Soc Smith, the guy I found in Baja California last April. His wife Jayne had hired me. He didn't know who I was, and I wanted to keep it that way. I didn't want to talk to him, find out if his voice was higher as Jayne said it would be when she got done with him. I got back to the bungalow at six and started to get ready for my date with Lil.

Eight

I'd put in a full day's work on the case and got to go surfing to boot. Now it was time to really start playing. I got as dressed up as I ever got, pressed chinos and a long sleeve, button down, burgundy stripe oxford shirt. I owned only one suit for whenever I had to appear in court. My regular attire for this time of the year was shorts and T-shirt. I'd been a beach bum for such a long time that I didn't even own a pair of dress shoes. I did have casual shoes, which I only wore with the suit, favoring instead fisherman's sandals or Topsiders with white crew socks. That night it was Topsiders. Lil, on the other hand, liked to dress up once in a while, and for being in her late fifties, she still had the figure of a woman who could wear sexy cocktail attire. And wear it she did that night. She put me to shame. I was greeted by the blond bombshell that she is, wearing a deep-purple silk mini skirt measured tastefully at lower thigh just above the knee with spaghetti straps accenting her smooth shoulders.

Lil and I had been intimate once upon a time, but the sparks just didn't fly, so we settled for being good friends and good neighbors. For one thing she was ten years older than I. Of course, nobody would have been able to tell that by looking at us that night. She actually looked younger than I with my craggy wind-blown surfer's face and my already-graying temples. I was sure she had some gray hair too, but she kept it well hid with whatever product she used to do that.

"Hey, Lil! Boy, don't you look good?"

My delight must have been obvious. She beamed.

"Well, thank you, Jack. You don't look half bad yourself. 'Fact I'd say you look pretty darn good."

It was a warm Indian summer evening, so nothing covered her shoulders, but she did carry a lightweight wrap for later and a small purple hand-bag that matched her dress. We walked the four blocks to the Santa Cruz Hotel.

"I talked to Dov Stein in his office this morning," I said as we walked.

"Did you learn anything useful for your investigation?"

"Hard to tell. One thing, he seemed overly offended when I mistakenly referred to a guy named Darryl Routh as a faculty member, and he wasn't. I thought Stein's rebuff was a bit strong. You know this guy Routh?"

"Never heard of him. Never got a haircut in my shop. I know all my people, and he's not one of them."

"I'm thinking Stein knows him better than he's letting on."

"Think so?"

"Yeah. I got my first glimpse of Routh today. Seems he's a regular at the Cooper House when there's music out front. Had lunch with Jean after I saw Stein and she filled in the blanks a little more. Anyway, I heard he hangs out at the Coop. when there's music, so I went looking for him this afternoon. He was out on the patio close to the band hangin' with some pasty-faced looking thug. Looks like a real preppy. A real Ivy League fraternity boy type. That's another one of the questions I keep asking. Why the hell did he ever come to a hippy school like U.C. Santa Cruz?"

"That's not so true anymore. Maybe ten years ago, yes, but not now."

"Really? How's that?"

"I've got this other client, a physics professor. He brought a pamphlet in the other day, something called 'Science Watch.' It rated the top ten universities in the country in physical and biological sciences, based on published papers in those two fields. Santa Cruz was number one in physical sciences. Harvard was second. Biological sciences Harvard was number one. Santa Cruz was in the top ten."

"Wow! I didn't know that."

"Also, nowadays you see more U.C. Santa Cruz students driving B.M.W.s and Mercedeses and fewer of them driving old beat up Volkswagen buses. I think the students are the same upper middle-class white kids from New York and Los Angeles mostly, but now they're more yuppie than the hippies who came before them."

"Yeah, well, this Darryl Routh is definitely more of a yuppie than he is a hippy."

Oh, Hard Tuesday

We walked up the steps to the front door of the restaurant and didn't have to wait long to get a table. Lil ordered a glass of white wine to go with her salmon dinner. I had red wine with my spaghetti and meatballs.

"Let's go over to the Oak Room instead of next door for our after-dinner drinks," I said as we ate. "Routh might still be hanging out there."

"Hey, what kind of a date is this, anyway?" she said. "You wan'a do some work, or enjoy the evening?"

"Enjoy the evening, of course. 'Fact, scratch that last suggestion. We'll go to the Red Room as planned."

And we did after we finished our dinners. There's a connecting door between the restaurant and the bar, and we went through it. This bar used to be a shrine for the Miss California contest, which was held at the Civic Auditorium until four years ago when it moved to San Diego. In the back area, there were pictures of various Miss Californias over the years, sashes, crowns and staffs, now gone, presumably to some bar in San Diego.

It was dark inside the bar, and it took my eyes a minute to adjust. There were five people at the bar, two guys right in the middle and a guy and two young women at the end. There were six other people scattered around the room at tables and in booths. It was the lull between happy hour and the Friday night rush.

"Don't look now," I said as my eyes adjusted. "That's Routh down at the end of the bar with the two women."

"Look like a couple of college girls," Lil said.

"Yeah, and I wonder where the big guy who was with him earlier is."

Neither of the two women was Karen. One of them could've been Rebecca Ginsberg. I hadn't seen a picture of her and didn't know what she looked like. I was guessing that neither of them was. All the descriptions I'd gotten so far of Rebecca told me she was more sophisticated than either of these two looked.

Lil and I found a booth in a secluded corner. I had a perfect view of Routh and the two ladies he seemed to be entertaining. He was doing most of the talking; the women seemed to be enjoying his rap. A cocktail waitress came over and took our order. Lil had a Margarita and I a shot of Glenlivet Scotch on the rocks.

Routh and the two women left shortly after Lil and I sat down. We only stayed for a half hour, long enough to finish our drinks. We didn't order a second. We'd both had a busy day and were tired, so we walked back to our places. We hugged and kissed before going into our respective houses.

Nine

Saturday was going to be another beautiful day, and I could tell before sunrise that it would be a hot one, too. The front patio of the Cooper House was going to be a busy place. I'd have to get there early if I wanted a seat on the side bench. Also, I wanted to get there before Routh. In fact, I wanted to be talking to David, if he was available, when Routh showed up. Give me some standing with the musicians. Not that I really cared about impressing the preppy boy, but I did want to get the upper hand on him.

I fixed some breakfast and ate as I looked at the morning paper. The first thing I checked was the tide chart on the weather page. Low tide was four hours ago, the middle of the night. There weren't going to be any waves breaking at five-thirty. No need to get out to West Cliff right away. I went ahead and finished my breakfast and read through the rest of the paper. The whole sports section was devoted to the Giants and A's and the World Series. The first game was to be played at the Oakland Coliseum later that day.

I finished breakfast and the paper, took a

shower, jumped on my bike and peddled out to West Cliff. Cowell's and Indicators were flat, but the Lane was decent. There were a few surfers in the water out at Middle Peak. I peddled out to the point and hung out for a while. It was pretty consistent, so the guys in the water were getting some sweet rides. There were a couple other guys, surfer types, standing a few feet away from me, watching.

"Whoa! Check it out! Go left!" one said looking at one of the guys getting up on a wave, but not loud enough for the guy to hear him.

"That was a good left," his buddy said.

"Yeah, but he missed it. It's okay. He did okay with the right. I just thought 'cause he's a goofy footer, yuh know?"

"Yeah, I know what yuh mean."

They were silent for a few minutes, watching the guys surfing.

"So, I seen Jasmine couple times now," one of them said.

"No kiddin'?"

"Pretty sweet!"

"Yeah! And thanks f'r tellin' me 'bout Natalie. Seen 'er twice 'n' she's great."

"Price's right too, huh?"

"Absolutely. How'd yuh meet 'em, anyway?"

"Grad. student up on campus turned me on. Said I wouldn't regret it and boy, I haven't."

"So, are the girls students?"

"I'm pretty sure they are. Workin' their way through college."

I heard enough to have a good idea what they were talking about. It was about time to head on home, still early enough to sit down at my keyboard and transcribe my notes on the case to the Word document in my Apple Computer before I made the trek to the Cooper House. I was absolutely going to include the conversation I'd just heard.

Ella Fitzgerald singing on the Cole Porter Songbook album I had on the C.D. player was background music while I worked. Just as I started wrapping things up on the computer, "Love for Sale" came on. Ella was so good, and that song, it seemed to me, was way ahead of its time. I thought that a song about prostitution, which was obviously the theme, was a pretty risqué topic for 1930 when it first appeared in the Broadway play *The New Yorkers*. Turned out it was perfect for the case I was working on.

At five to twelve, I headed out the door. It took me ten minutes to walk to the Cooper House. The band had just started playing. Don, the leader, was on vibes, Bill McCord on drums, James Monroe on bass, David O'Connor on guitar, Don's son Donny on tenor sax, and "three-finger" Frank Castellanos on congas. David Barnes hadn't arrived yet. Nobody was sitting on the side bench, so I went right over to it and grabbed the seat closest to the band, the one Pasty Face was sitting in yesterday. The waitress brought me a Perrier as the band played the Duke Ellington/Billy Strayhorn tune "Satin Doll."

David showed up at five to one as the band was closing out the first set. He sat next to me as the band members went off in different directions to get sandwiches at Zoccoli's and Heinz Beer Garden.

"Doesn't look like your guy's showed up yet," David said.

"So far, no. But, yuh know, I saw 'im last night at the Red Room."

"Really? What happened?"

"Nothin' really. Took my neighbor to dinner at the Santa Cruz Hotel. Went next door for after-dinner drinks, and he was there at the bar."

"Your next-door neighbor, the barber?"

"Yup. I didn't talk to 'im, though. He was busy with a couple a' young beauties. Looked like coeds."

"Looks like yuh won't have long to wait now," David said, pointing to Routh and his pasty-faced friend on the sidewalk, heading toward the entrance to the patio. "Here he comes right now."

Routh looked like he was enjoying the pleasant afternoon; he walked with a carefree gait. He smiled and nodded at the people he passed, and if he passed a pretty young woman, he made a bigger display than he did with the others. Pasty Face, on the other hand, looked weight-lifter stiff, uptight, like he had a steel rod up his ass. More ominous even than his bearing was his hard, unsmiling stare in my direction. Even though he was wearing shades I could tell he was looking straight at me. His mouth wasn't smiling either. All of which was completely incongruous with what he was wearing—canary yellow spandex pants with white shoes, matching belt again, and an orange shirt with a big open collar. Quite the dresser. Routh by contrast was dressed like the preppy boy he was—khaki chinos and short sleeve sport shirt, not unlike how he was dressed the day before.

"Wow!" said David. "Get a load outa' the look Blondie's givin' yuh, and check out his threads."

"I noticed."

They came onto the patio and right over to the bench where we were sitting. They sat at the table next to ours, the one the black guy was sitting at yesterday. Pasty Face kept staring hard at me while Routh nodded and smiled, first at David, then me. The band started to assemble with their instruments, so David got up and headed toward the bandstand.

"Do 'Angel Eyes,'" I said as he moved off.

"Okay," he said.

The tables closest to the band were by now all filled with diners and drinkers. The ones on the other side of the patio entrance were about half full.

David stepped up to the microphone and said, "Here's a special tune for a special friend, 'Angel Eyes.'"

As soon as he started singing, both Routh and Pasty Face lit up. There was a very slight breeze that was blowing their smoke right at me. I'm a lifelong non-smoker who is a worse anti-smoker than any ex-smoker you're ever going to meet. It comes from having been raised by a three-pack-a-day Camel-smoking dad and a mom who smoked just under a pack a day. What I object to most is the stink. Pipe and cigar smokers aren't a problem because all they're smoking is tobacco. The latest research shows that tobacco companies are putting all kinds of additives in cigarettes, like nicotine enhancers, that really make them stink, and probably make them harder on your health, too. And then there's the litter problem. Cigarette smokers flick their ashes wherever they're standing, and how often do you see cigarette butts (not even butts, but expended filters) discarded on sidewalks, in storm gutters and in planters? And how ridiculous do people look standing on the street or sitting at a table blowing smoke out of their mouths and noses?

"You fella's wan'a trade places with me?" I said. "I'm getting your secondhand smoke here with this breeze."

Pasty Face, who was still looking aggressively and pissed off at me, took a big drag from his Marlboro, blew the smoke in my direction and started to stand up in a hostile way, but Routh touched his arm, and he sat back down.

"We'll just put 'em out," he smiled and mashed out his own. "Come on, Downs," he said to his partner. "Put it out."

"Thanks," I said, thinking I'd have to call Jean again first thing Monday morning and find out what I could about Pasty Face now that I had a name.

"Hey, no problem."

David finished "Angel Eyes" and started "Guess I'll Hang My Tears Out To Dry" as the applause died down. He really does sound a lot like Frank Sinatra. Preppy Boy and Pasty Face ordered a couple bottles of Beck's. As soon as Pasty Face paid the tab, I got right down to it with Routh.

"You're Darryl Routh, right?" I asked.

"Yeah. Do I know you?" he said, looking a little taken aback.

"Well, no. We haven't met, but I know who

you are."

"Really. How?"

"I'm looking for Karen Babbit, and your name came up in my inquiry. Yuh know she's missing." I knew he knew. That's why it wasn't a question. "Her family is eager to find her. You wouldn't have any information about that, would you?"

"Now, why would you think I'd know anything about that?"

His use of the specific pronoun told me he knew everything about it.

"A couple people I've spoken to said you and she're pretty close."

"You're talking to the wrong people. I know her from up on campus, but I wouldn't say I'm close to her. She was in one class I taught. That's it."

Pasty Face pretended not to hear our conversation, but I knew he heard every word. We couldn't whisper because of the music, but we weren't exactly talking loud either. He sat stone-faced, only periodically picking up his bottle of Beck's and sipping it. I knew Routh was lying to me; I came prepared for it. His pleasant smile was gone, and his brow was wrinkled. He knew a lot more than he was telling me.

"Didn't you also live across the hall from her at the Palomar?"

"Well, yeah, but I hardly ever saw her."

"How 'bout acting as unofficial counselor to her on campus? You ever do any of that?"

"You're giving me way too much credit for things I never had authority or qualifications to do. I was only a graduate lecturer, not a counselor. I don't even know who Miss Babbit's counselor was. Where do you get this stuff, anyway?"

I ignored his question and pushed forward.

"What kind of a grade did she get in your class?"

"Don't remember, exactly. Probably an A. I think everybody in that class got an A."

"Really? They all got A's?"

My disbelief was obvious, had to be, even to someone as clueless as Routh. I didn't want to overplay my hand by thinking he wasn't smart, but then his involvement in the petty crimes of his past would indicate that he couldn't have had too much on the ball. And how smart can you be to give every kid in your class an A. You're either stupid or lazy or both.

"I think so," was his only response to my question.

He was back to smiling his smug grin, so I quit talking, for now. Everything he'd said to me was a direct contradiction to what I'd heard from Lisa, Stein and Jason, especially about his closeness to Karen.

It was pretty obvious I wasn't going to get anything from Routh, so I didn't say anymore for the remainder of Warmth's set. When the break came, David and I joined a couple band members in the stained-glass enclosure in the easement between the Cooper House and the Neary Building next door. Those guys liked to go back there and smoke a joint. I joined them, but I didn't smoke with them, not because I was uptight about it, because I wasn't, not like I was about cigarettes. I still had some work to do on the case, and I wanted my head to be clear to do it, so when the band went back to work, I headed home. As I walked away from the Cooper House, I turned to see Routh sitting at the table I'd just vacated. The seat I was sitting in was vacant. I didn't see Pasty Face anywhere.

Ten

One reason I'm a successful investigator is because of a gift, a sixth sense, if you will—the ability to know when someone's following me or when someone's lying to me or not telling me everything. The sense had kicked in on meeting Danielle and taking this case. She was holding out on me all right, but why and what was it? Stein and Jordon were holding something back, too. I didn't know what it was either. Each one of those people had his or her own reasons for doing it, and I wasn't going to find out what they were until Karen turned up. The three coeds were the only ones I was sure were telling me everything they knew.

The sixth sense was kicking in again as I walked from the Cooper House to my bungalow. Someone was following me. I really couldn't look back to check without getting caught in the act by whoever it was, but when I made my left turn at the corner of Church and Center, I took a quick glance back up Church and just missed seeing a figure moving into the alcove of the *Sentinel* building. I could have sworn I saw the cuff of a pair of canary yellow pants and a white shoe. The newspaper office was closed.

As I was passing Lil's place, I saw her in the front window, talking to a client who was standing next to her chair. She saw me and motioned me in. I went left onto her walkway, gave a quick glance back up Center Street, and saw no one on the side-walks or in the street. She closed her blinds as I went in the unlocked front door. The client nodded in my direction on his way out. She started cleaning her tools and putting them away. She'd just finished her last haircut of the day. This was the start of her weekend.

"So, were you able to talk to Mr. Routh?" she asked.

"Yeah, but I didn't find out much. Didn't find out anything about Karen. Did find out Preppy Boy's a liar, but I pretty much knew that goin' in. Denied everything Stein and the other witnesses told me, and I'm more inclined to believe them, especially the three girls on Lincoln Street."

"So, what's your next move?"

"God, I'm really not sure. I've got three different people telling me that Karen and Routh were close, and Routh saying it's not true. And, so what? The real question is: where's Karen and what exactly is she up to?"

"Didn't you say Jean clued you in on Routh's record? Does he have a record?"

"Yeah."

"How bad is it? Get arrested?"

"Twice. Brandishing a firearm and pander-ing."

"Pandering! There yuh go. Didn't you say Karen was shopping at Camouflage for sexy under-wear?"

"Oh, I get it. You think she's hookin' and Routh's her pimp?"

"Why not?"

"I thought about that, but I didn't wan'a be-lieve it. Yuh know, maybe that conversation I over-heard on the cliff this morning might have some-thing to do with all of this."

I told her about the two guys I heard talking at the Lane.

"'Sounds like it has everything to do with it."

If anybody knew anything about prostitution in Santa Cruz, it was Lil. Not firsthand, but as an observer. Before she bought the house and set up her business there, she was working in a barber sa-lon on Forty-first Avenue on the Opal Cliffs side of the railroad tracks. It was only a two-chair shop, the Trojan Palace, occupying about a quarter of the front of the building. The back three-quarters was a bordello, Helen's Den. The lady who worked the first chair ran the whole operation. She was the bar-ber out front and the madam in back. I never went there for a haircut, so I'm not really sure what the setup was. Lil worked the second chair until she got her journeyman's license. One of her customers was a banker, and he basically told her to find some place to move her business to. He said he'd get her a loan. Telling her it didn't look good, he said he couldn't keep going to the Trojan Palace for his haircuts. So, he got her a home loan and she bought the house next door to me.

"You got a *Good Times* in here?" I said, moving over to the table where her magazines and newspapers were stacked.

Good Times is a weekly free newspaper, more of an entertainment guide, that comes out on Thursdays. Lil had the latest edition in with her magazines. I opened it to the want ads. There were two columns of massage ads—one for therapeutic massage and one for what looked like sexual massage. My index finger scrolled down the sexual massage column, and there it was, one ad for Natalie and Jasmine. Suddenly, the want ads page from the *Sentinel* in Routh's room yesterday came to mind. I hadn't looked closely to see if this ad was listed in the massage column. I'd look at my copy when I got home to see if it was there.

"Here, check this out," I said to Lil, pointing at the ad. "It's the same two names those surfers mentioned this morning. I'm guessing their real names are Rebecca Ginsberg and Karen Babbit. Wha'da yuh think?"

"Could be. The girls out at Helen's all used stage names."

"Can I keep this *Good Times?*"

"Sure. You go'n'a call the number? Set up an appointment?"

"Probably. Seems to be the best way to find out if Karen's one of these two women. Hey, yuh wan'a go to breakfast at Gilda's tomorrow morning?"

"Wow! Twice in one week. Are we dating again?"

"I don't know. Are we?"

"I'd love to go to Gilda's for breakfast. What

time?"

"Let's make it early. How 'bout I come over to your place at seven and we leave then? We'll be there plenty early to beat the crowds."

"'Sounds good. See yuh then."

She finished cleaning up her shop, and I went home. I cut out the whole massage column from the *Good Times* want ads and put it in the file on Karen Babbit. Then I dug up yesterday's *Sentinel* and looked at the massage column. Sure enough, there was the same ad for Natalie and Jasmine. I cut that column out too and put it in the file.

Eleven

The phone rang at about two-thirty. Lil's halting and weak voice came on the line.

"…Jack…h-help…I'm hurt," she said in a thin, shaky voice. "…come…quick."

I hung up, pulled on a pair of trousers and hurried next door. When I got to the front porch, the door was ajar, the frame where it latched and locked, broken and splintered. I went in. Lil was sitting slumped in her barber chair. The whole left side of her face was bruised. Her forehead on that side had a vertical cut to the eyebrow. Her left eye was black and blue, and that cheek was swollen.

"What happened?" I asked helping her to her feet. "Let's get you back in bed."

"…heard someone…t-tampering with my front door…tryin'…tryin' to get in…got up to see…door flew open…knocked me down…."

"You see what he looked like?"

"…ski mask…couldn't tell…."

"We better get you an ambulance. Get yuh out to Dominican. I'll call 911."

I picked up her phone and dialed.

"911 emergency."

"Yeah, this is Jack Lefevre and I'm at 512 Center Street, Downtown Santa Cruz. We're go'n'a need an ambulance out here. My next-door neighbor, Lil Gillis, has been assaulted in her own home."

"Is she conscious?"

"Yes, she is, but I think she's in shock. We really need that ambulance in a hurry, and get the cops out here, too."

I hung up and went in to sit with Lil as we waited for the ambulance.

"Anything else you can tell me about the guy?" I said.

"...not really...kept saying, '...where is he?'...southern accent...d-didn't know what he was talkin' 'bout...."

The fire department, only two blocks away, was the first to arrive, red lights flashing in the night. Three big, strapping firemen got out of the truck and came into the house. I pointed them to the bedroom. Shortly after they started to minister to her, the ambulance arrived. When I got out to the front porch to greet them, I noticed a couple of the neighbors in bathrobes on their front porches watching the action.

The paramedics went into the house and stood by as the firemen were looking Lil over and asking her questions. Without turning his attention away from examining her eyes, the fireman said calmly to the paramedics, "Get a stretcher in here. We're go'n'a send Lil here to emergency." They went out to the ambulance and got a foldout gurney from the back. They rolled it into the house as the firemen were finishing their examination and questions. They lifted Lil off her bed and onto the gurney and wrapped her in a warm blanket. I followed them out, and after they got her into the ambulance, they drove off, red lights still flashing. I closed her door as best I could, got into my car and headed out to Dominican Hospital. I wasn't paying any attention to the speed limit, so it didn't surprise me that I caught up with the ambulance on Soquel Avenue just before it crossed the bridge to the hospital. I followed it the rest of the way to the emergency ward. I was at Lil's side as they wheeled her through the double doors.

"Sir, you can wait right over there," said the receiving nurse, pointing to a waiting area with magazine laden tables and chairs.

I wanted to call Lil's daughter, but I didn't have her number, so I let it slide. There was no one else in the waiting room with me, so I just sat there alone, thinking, *what happened?* I had a good idea who it was. The first person who came to mind was Preppy Boy's pasty face friend, Downs. He was big and strong enough to kick a door in and knock someone as little as Lil over like that. Everything I'd heard and my own brief encounter with Routh told me he certainly didn't have either the strength or the salt to do it.

I was thinking about calling Charles Van Houten after sunup. Not that I couldn't handle Pasty Face on my own. I could. I just wanted Charles by my side for backup, and he'd want to be there. After all he was a regular in Lil's shop.

He was one of the meanest guys I ever met. A

wiry little guy, about five-nine, a hundred fifty. Tough as a junkyard dog. A mean motor scooter. Born and raised in Birmingham, Alabama, Charles had a completely contrary personality to many southern whites who grew up in the fifties and six-ties. He kept up a strong southern accent, which he flaunted. His parents were both conservative south-erners who believed strongly in racial segregation. None of it rubbed off on Charles. As soon as he turned eighteen, he joined two organizations, the N.A.A.C.P. and the Communist Party, in that order. In 1963, that was making a statement. He was much more dialed into the civil rights movement than he was communist politics. Every year he attended the N.A.A.C.P. picnic on Labor Day at De Laveaga Park. Last year he was a Jesse Jackson delegate to the Democratic Convention. He hung out at a cou-ple of the alkie bars in downtown, where on more than one occasion, he told me how he'd braced some redneck who used the word "nigger."

Charles was tough. His favorite quote was, "You don't spell bad B-I-G." You damn sure didn't want him as an enemy. He worked at an unassum-ing job as an analyst in the County Administrative Office. The job was quite ordinary, but Charles made the most of it politically. He knew all the im-portant players and had a good relationship with the principal members of the Board of Supervisors.

As I thought about Charles and Lil, Routh and Pasty Face, a policeman entered, went up to the nurse's desk and asked for Lil. I approached as the nurse was pointing him in the right direction. His nametag said T. Nally.

"Hi, Officer Nally," I said as I came up to him. "I'm Jack Lefevre. I called it in, and then I followed the ambulance out here. Lil's my next-door neighbor."

"Really. What do you know about the incident?"

"Not much. It happened a little after two, about an hour ago. I was the first one on the scene. She called me and I rushed right over."

"Okay. Come with me while I talk to her. Maybe you can fill in any missing pieces."

I followed him into the ward, where there were about ten beds separated by curtains. Most of the beds were occupied. When we got to Lil, a doctor was ministering to her. She was still conscious, and a lot more alert than she had been an hour ago. The doctor was just getting ready to administer a sedative.

"Would it be all right to ask her a couple questions, Doctor?" Officer Nally asked.

"I think so," said the doctor. "I'll hold off on this till you finish."

He took the syringe away and left the little curtained cubicle. Lil was sitting up in the hospital bed and was looking alert. Her injuries were more bruises than cuts. It didn't appear that she needed any stitches. The doctor had put a butterfly bandage on the cut on her forehead.

"Can you tell me anything about the person who attacked you?"

"He was big. Wore a ski mask, so I really couldn't describe what he looked like. Blue eyes. Wore dark clothing, a turtleneck, no gloves. He was white, what I'd call abnormally white. Like maybe he was an albino. No color in his hands."

The more I heard, the more it sounded like Routh's friend ol' Pasty Face.

"That's good," said Officer Nally. "Anything else you can remember?"

"He must've yelled at me three times, 'Where is he?' That was after he'd looked in every room in the house. Sounded like a southern accent to me. High pitched voice. Didn't know what he was talking about."

I hadn't heard Pasty Face talk, so I didn't know if he had a southern accent or not. If he did, that would be another good reason to bring Charles into it.

"Anything else about his appearance? Height? Weight? Roughly."

"He was big. Bigger'n Jack. I'd say six feet or more. He was pretty trim. Somewhere around a couple hundred pounds. Hard to tell, though, with the way he was dressed."

"And you say all he did was look in the rooms?" Officer Nally asked. "Didn't take anything? Wasn't searching for anything?"

"Didn't look like it."

"And you don't have any idea who it might've been."

"No, sir."

"You?" This to me.

"No, sir," I lied, but it wasn't really a lie, since I wasn't absolutely sure it was Pasty Face. The more I thought about it, the more I thought it was he who'd done it. Now I was pretty sure he'd followed me home from the Cooper House yester-day. He saw me go into Lil's place and thought it was where I lived. He didn't know I was in the house next door. I was definitely go'n'a call Jean Monday morning. Get a line on this character.

"Okay," Nally said. "I'll write this report and file it. If anything else comes to mind, give me a call."

He handed both of us his card and left. The doctor came back into the curtained cubicle carry-ing the syringe.

"We're going to send you home, Lil. This is something to relax you so you can get some sleep for what's left of the night. You don't have a con-cussion. More bruised and battered than anything. Take one aspirin every four hours for the rest of the day, and you should be okay."

"You wan'a call your daughter, tell her what happened?" I said to Lil when we got back to her place.

"Oh, no. It's too late, and she'll only want to come over. Let her sleep. I'll call her in the morn-ing."

"Okay."

I finally got her back into her own bed by four-thirty. I curled up on her couch, and we both slept until almost ten o'clock.

Twelve

I got up off the couch, stepped to the front window, opened the blinds and looked out at the congregation filing into the little wooden Baptist church across the street. Lil still wasn't up and about. Most of the congregation was black, and were they ever dressed to the nines! I turned away from the window and went into the kitchen to put on a pot of coffee. There was flour in a canister on the kitchen counter and milk and eggs in the refrigerator. She had baking powder in the spice drawer. I made pancakes.

Lil was moving around behind the closed door of her bedroom, and then water was running in the shower. I went ahead and whipped up a batch of pancakes, stacking them on a metal tray in the oven. She came out just as I used up the last of the pancake batter. The left side of her face was swollen, the butterfly bandage was still on the lump on her forehead, and she had a black eye. She wasn't wearing any makeup, and she hadn't blown her hair dry. It was wet and combed straight back.

"Boy, that's a nasty bruise you've got there."

"Yes, I know," and just as she said it, she put

her face into my shoulder and started to cry.

"Yeah, I know. Feelings're hurt more'n anything. Right?"

"Well, yeah. But most of all, my head hurts." By now she was sobbing. "Why would anybody do something like this to me?"

"Don't worry. I'm go'n'a find out, and whoever it was is go'n'a be one sorry son of a bitch. Sorry he ever laid eyes on you. 'Fact I think I know who it is. It obviously wasn't a robbery, or he would've taken something. Didn't you say he kept asking you where somebody was?"

"Yes. What do you think he meant by that?"

"Not sure, but I think he was asking you where I was. Thought this was my house. Don't worry about it. I'm go'n'a find out today. Now come on. Let's have some pancakes and try to forget about this for now. Mine aren't as good as Gilda's, but they'll do."

She grabbed a napkin from the table and dried her tears. Before we sat down to pancakes, she got on the phone and called her daughter. She didn't pick up so Lil left a message on her machine.

When we finished eating, she gathered up the dishes and took them to the kitchen sink. I gave her a big, strong hug, and, what I hoped, was a reassuring smile. Then I went back over to my place and took a shower. After my shower I called Charles.

"Hey, what's happenin'?" I said when he picked up.

"Not much what're you up?"

"Got a little problem here. Somebody broke into Lil's house last night."

"No kiddin'."

It wasn't a question. Not for Charles. Most of the time with him it was a statement.

"No kiddin'. Happened 'bout two-thirty this morning. Heard the guy trying to jimmy her door. Got up to check it out. Asshole kicked the damn door in. Hit her right in the face."

"She okay? Know who it was?"

That was the only time it would be a question for Charles. When he was inquiring about someone's wellbeing, it was a serious question. And it was especially serious when it concerned someone as special to him as Lil.

"Yeah, she's okay. Black eye. Swollen cheek. Small cut and bump on the head. Otherwise okay. No concussion. Nothing like that. Got an idea who it was."

"Really."

"What're yuh doin' this afternoon?"

"I'm helpin' you find this fucker. Meet yuh at your place. Tell me what time."

"How 'bout one o'clock?"

"See yuh then."

We disconnected, and I went back over to Lil's house with my toolbox to check out her front door, make up a list of stuff to pick up at San Lorenzo Lumber to fix it. She was back in bed, resting. The doorjamb was splintered, the striker plate torn off. After I finished putting my list together, I drove over to the lumberyard to pick up supplies. Back at Lil's place, she was awake again and her daughter was there. So, I sat with them until Charles showed up at one o'clock.

Oh, Hard Tuesday

The first thing he did was give Lil a big hug and told her we were going to find the asshole who'd done this to her. Thus reassured, she smiled and hugged him stronger than he'd done her.

He and I went over to my house to talk strategy. I told him the whole story from the beginning when Danielle called me on Thursday up until yesterday when I thought Pasty Face was following me home from the Cooper House.

"I got an idea what y'all're thinking," Charles said in his in-your-face Alabama accent. "We're goin' after these motherfuckers."

"Yes, we are. They're go'n'a be hanging at the Coop. this afternoon. Wha'da yuh say we go pay 'em a visit?"

"'Sounds good. I c'n hardly wait."

"It's what, one-fifteen? They showed up about one o'clock yesterday. Made it there ahead of 'em; want 'em to get settled in before we show up today. We should get there around quarter to two, 'bout the time the band takes a break."

"Okay. We got about twenty minutes. You got a plan."

"Yeah. What we'll do is you drive your car over to the parking structure across the street from the *Sentinel* and park upstairs. Get down to the Cooper House and make a pass on the sidewalk, scope 'em out. They'll be sitting on the side under the windows of the bar. You can't miss 'em if they're there." I showed him the mug shot Jean had given me. "You can see here Routh's a mealy mouth little preppy, and his buddy's a big guy, white-blond hair and pasty face, same shade. Dresses pretty flashy. After you've eyeballed 'em, go back up to your car and disappear. You know how you do it. Then I'm go'n'a go get 'em to take a walk with me. We'll be going up the car ramp, not the stairs. You'll be there, out of sight."

"You got it."

"I really don't expect anything more'n words to fly, but just in case."

"You got it," he repeated.

Thirteen

As I walked alongside Gottschalks at the corner of Pacific and Church, I caught my first glimpse of the two punks across the street at the Cooper House. Tweedley Dee and Tweedley Dum. It was all I could do to keep my rage under control. And the closer I got to them, the harder it was to manage it, especially when I was close enough to see Routh's usual shit-eatin' grin. Pasty Face sat next to him like a stone, dour, once again dressed like he'd just come in from a round of golf.

The band was playing the last number of the set, "What's New." David was doing the vocals.

The moment Routh caught sight of me, his smile faded. His buddy's expression was unchanged behind his shades. I stood next to the tree in the brick planter on the sidewalk. When Routh and I made eye contact (his shades were a lighter tint than his pal's, so I could see when he looked at me), I smiled and nodded in his direction. I pointed my right index finger at him and cocked my thumb down and up in pantomime, aiming and shooting at him. He frowned some more. Pasty Face stared straight ahead, I think. Because his shades were so dark, it was impossible to see which way he was looking, but like yesterday, I could tell he was looking straight at me. More like drilling me with his stare.

"'T's happenin', Jack," David said as he approached at the end of the set.

"Not much. Just checkin' out our boy. Think I'll go have a chat with 'im," I said, not taking my eyes off Routh.

"Didn't get what yuh needed yesterday, huh?"

"Not by a long shot. 'Fact, today it's go'n'a be different."

"I'll let yuh get to it. I'm goin' up to Zoc's, for a pastrami."

"See yuh later," I said, still not taking my eyes off Routh.

David headed off to Zoccoli's, and I went into the Cooper House patio and headed straight over to Routh.

"I wan'a talk to you," I said with what I hoped was a tough-guy snarl in my voice. It wouldn't do to be any other way at this point. I was pissed!

Before Routh could respond, Pasty Face stood up, moved in close and said in a high-pitched, but not-loud, voice in a southern accent,

"Whyn't y'all fuck off."

I held my ground, looking straight at Routh. Staring into his eyes was like looking into a vacuum. I saw there an emptiness that left me wondering if they were scared or belligerent. I'd bet on the former.

"Let's take a walk."

I knew he'd go along. He thought he'd get me

alone, and his friend'd jump me. And sure enough, he confirmed it.

"Mind if my friend joins us?"

"Ain't go'n'a make it any easier. Do what yuh want."

It was then that I finally looked at Tweedley Dum. His shades were a little too dark for me to read anything in his eyes. I could see them at this short distance, but barely. We headed out onto the sidewalk and across the street.

"Where we goin'?" Routh said.

"Parking garage."

I detected a slight smile. It was unlike his characteristic smirk, more a smile of satisfaction. He thought he had me.

We headed down Church Street a block to the double-deck parking structure. As soon as we got up to the second level, I could feel Charles' presence. I couldn't see him but I knew he was close. We stopped just inside the car ramp on the second deck. Still smiling, I spoke first.

"So, who the fuck yuh think you're messin' with, sonny boy?"

"I don't…," he started, but I cut him off.

"Don't fuckin' talk, asshole. I'm not finished here."

Just then his buddy made his move, but before he could even get close to me, Charles was all over him. It was almost comical watching little, wiry Charles beating the shit out of this guy who was so much bigger. Popeye versus Brutus. It was when Charles had Pasty Face well in hand that I grabbed Routh by his shirtfront and braced him against a car.

"Listen here, you little fuckin' asshole. Anything else happens to me or my next door neighbor—yeah don't try to fuckin' deny it 'cause I know your goon here broke into her place last night and roughed 'er up—I'm comin' after both a' your sorry asses, and when that happens, you'll rue the fuckin' day you ever laid eyes on me. 'Fact I haven't even decided if I'll just do it anyway. You're on notice."

With that, I let go of his shirt, and Charles was at my side. Downs was out cold between two cars. We walked over to the stairs and went down to the street.

"Boy, you sure took care a' that guy!" I said as we walked.

"Yeah. Couldn't help it. He was pretty slow."

"I guess! Those assholes're punks. Big guy's a bully. Prob'ly couldn't win a fair fight. Routh's nothin' but the kind a' candy ass Pasty Face'd get the most fun outa' bullyin'."

"We're goin' after 'em again. Tell me when."

"I've got'a figure out a few things first. Then I'll go have a chat with Routh. Just him and me. Can't be distracted from my main goal, and that's to find Karen Babbit. Yuh know, revenge is never a good reason to go after anybody."

"You're right. Maybe I'll just take care of it myself."

"Don't tell me about it."

"I'm go'n'a go back, keep an eye on 'em, find out where ol' Pasty Face lives. He's the only one I'm interested in 'cause a' Lil. I don't much give a shit about the other asshole."

"Like I said, don't tell me about it."

Oh, Hard Tuesday

I headed back to my place and got into some work clothes. I grabbed my woodworking tools and a couple of sawhorses and went next door.

Fourteen

By the time I got to Lil's, her daughter was gone, and she was resting quietly, but as soon as I started working, she came out and kept me company.

"So, is there something you know about this you're not telling me?" she asked as I measured the doorjamb.

I knew what she meant by "this," and didn't respond to her question, but she wasn't letting me off the hook. She persisted.

"I could tell by the look on your face last night when the police officer asked if you knew anything and you said no. I bet you know a lot more than you're letting on. And what were you and Charles doing just now?"

"Okay, okay. You know me better'n I know myself. I'm ninety-nine percent sure I know who it is."

"Does it have anything to do with this missing person case you're working on?"

"Pretty sure."

"Tell me."

"'Member yesterday me telling you about a

guy named Darryl Routh? Guy we saw at the Red Room Friday night? You suggested he might be pimping for the two missing women. Well, he's got this pasty-faced goon he hangs around with. 'Member how you told the cop how white the guy who attacked you was? Pretty sure it was ol' Pasty Face. Fits the description. Followed me home yesterday. Must've seen me come into your house. Thought it was my house, and that's why he broke in. He was after me."

"Wow! Isn't that cute!"

"Not really when you think about it. Adds up. These two punks are into this thing, whatever it is, up to their eyeballs. Didn't take long after I started asking Routh about Karen Babbit before Pasty Face went into action."

"Does seem planned, not too coincidental."

"Not at all coincidental."

"So why didn't you say something to the policeman?"

"Come on. You know me better'n that. You asked what Charles and I were doin' just now? We were talkin' to those two assholes. Well, I was anyway. Talkin' to Routh. Charles came out of the shadows and had a little more intimate conversation with Pasty Face. He *was* pissed!"

"This guy got a name?"

"All I know is Downs. That's what I heard Routh call 'im. Don't know if it's his first name or last."

She didn't ask for details on what Charles had done to him, and I didn't offer any. I worked pretty steadily through the afternoon, and around four-thirty, the job was done except for the paint. I left that for Lil.

"You feel up to goin' out to the wharf for dinner?" I said. "Riva, Stagnaro's or maybe you've got a suggestion? We got'a make up for missing breakfast out there this morning."

"Are you kiddin'? I'm always up for going to either of those two places. You pick it. What time?"

"How 'bout six o'clock?"

"'Sounds delightful. I'll see you then."

I went back to my place and cleaned up. As I passed the office after my shower, I saw the red light blinking on the phone. I went on into the bedroom and got dressed. Then I checked the phone message. It was Charles.

"Call me," he said in his characteristic Alabama accent. "I got something f'r y'all on those two guys."

There was still time before I had to meet Lil, so I dialed Charles' number, and he picked up before the first ring. Or so it seemed. He was quick.

"Wha'cha got?"

"I got lucky. When I split with you, they were just going down the stairs of the parking structure. Must've taken Pasty Face some time to come to. Followed 'em on foot over to the Palomar. Then I got my car and staked 'em out for about twenty minutes. When they came out, looked like Preppy Boy cleaned up ol' Pasty Face quite a bit. Followed 'em over to that other garage by Front and River. They drove out to a townhouse on Chanticleer. They hung out in the car for a while. Looked like they were waitin' for someone or somethin'. Then an older gentleman came out the front door of the unit those guys went into after he was gone. Didn't look like he saw them. They got out of their car after he drove away. Want me to tell you what he looked like?"

"Absolutely."

"He was wearing a snap-brim fedora, but I saw he was gray at the temples. Hat almost looked like a disguise. He had a full beard, same gray as his sideburns. White shirt and tie, tweed jacket with leather patches on the elbows. Wire-rim glasses. You know someone fits that description?"

He had described Dr. Dov Stein right down to the leather patches on his jacket.

"That's Stein. Yuh know? The prof.?"

"No kiddin'. Y'er two punks were met at the front door by a beautiful young brunette with a big smile. Didn't stay long. Maybe fifteen minutes. Pasty Face was doin' all the driving. He parked back in the structure on Front and River Extension. That's when they split up. Preppy Boy went down Front toward the Palomar. I followed Pasty Face to the Saint George. Desolation row. I got a friend lives there. One of my drinkin' buddies over at Bei's. I followed Pasty Face in. His room was down the hall from my friend's room. Number's 214."

"You get the address of the townhouse?"

"Sure did. Nine-twenty-five, unit four."

"One more question. What kind a' car were they drivin'?"

"Late model maroon Chevy Blazer. Personalized plate: T-R-I-X."

"All right. Thanks, Charles. This helps a lot.

And I'm glad you didn't jump the bastard again."

"I ain't done yet."

He hung up and I finished getting ready.

"After we split up today," I said to Lil as we ate at Stagnaro's, "Charles went back and followed Routh and Pasty Face. One who attacked you lives at the Saint George."

"Really?"

"Seems incongruous."

"Incongruous?"

"I didn't tell you how he dresses?"

"No."

"He wears stuff like lime green spandex with white shoes and belt. How many people you see hanging in the lobby of the George dressed like that? Salvation Army's more their speed."

"I see what you mean."

"Before he followed 'em home, he tracked 'em out to a townhouse on Chanticleer. I think that's where the two women are turning tricks. You were probably right when you said Routh was pimping for 'em. And guess who came out of the townhouse before Routh and his goon went in?"

"Let me guess. Dov Stein."

"You got that right."

"You going out there to check on it?"

"Maybe Tuesday. Tomorrow morning I'm go'n'a call Jean. See what I can find out about Pasty Face. See if he's got a sheet. I've only got one name on the guy, Downs, and I don't know if it's his first name or last. After Jean gets back to me, I'm goin' back up to campus and have another chat with Stein. The last thing I'll do tomorrow is call the number in the paper. Set up an appointment for Tuesday. If it's the same address Charles gave me, I'll know it's the missing women, and I'll know that both Stein and Routh've been lying to me all along. Then I'll go out and have a talk with Karen. See if I can find out what's on her mind."

We finished our dinners and went home. After tucking Lil in, I went to my place and worked on my schedule for Monday.

Fifteen

I waited till nine-thirty to call Jean. That gave her time to settle into her office and get any business she might have with Jenkins out of the way. She picked up on the first ring.

"Jean Kaiser."

"How yuh doin', doll?"

"Not too b-a-d. How're you?"

"Could be better. Lil next door had a break-in late Saturday night. Guy roughed 'er up."

"Really? Didn't hear about that one! Have to check it out!"

"Do. And while you're at it, check out someone else for me. Name's Downs. That's all I have. Don't know if it's a first name or last name. I also got a plate, vanity: T-R-I-X. Guy hangs around with Darryl Routh. Looks like muscle, and I'd bet he's got a sheet."

"You think he might've been the one who roughed up Lil?"

"Let's say he's a prime suspect. Fits the description Lil gave Officer Nally when he interviewed her. You know him?"

"Yes. Tom. Good guy. You give him the

guy's name?"

"Actually, no. I wasn't sure it was him at the time I talked with the officer."

There was a pause on the other end of the line as Jean processed what I'd just said. I knew she was thinking my story was a little fishy.

"Wish I could see your eyes right now," she said. "I think I'd see some dissembling in them."

"Dissembling?"

"Come on. You know perfectly well what I mean."

"You 'n' Lil," I said, shaking my head. "You know me better'n I know myself. Let's just say I was pretty positive when Lil described him to Nally. She didn't give 'im much. He was completely covered. Ski mask, dark turtleneck, but no gloves. She said his hands were as white as a kitchen range. I thought of Pasty Face right away, but I didn't wan'a say anything to the officer because I wanted to check it out for myself."

"Jack! What are you talking about? What, or should I say, who is 'Pasty Face'?"

"Pasty Face is Downs, and I really need to know more about 'im."

"I hope you're not thinking about any retribution here. You need to report what you know and let the police handle it."

"Don't worry. Retribution's not my aim. I'm looking for a missing person, and I'm positive this guy knows something about it. I've only talked to Routh once since the attack, and it was civil. Pasty Face was there, and he wasn't a problem. Only way I'll deal with him again is if *he* starts something."

I didn't tell her the part about Charles kicking the guy's ass, but I did tell her the whole story all the way up to and including the part about Charles seeing Stein coming out of the townhouse on Chanticleer and then Routh and Downs going in.

"I'm go'n'a be headin' outa' here 'bout a quarter to eleven. Goin' back up to campus. Have another chat with Stein. I think I've got this thing figured out. The women aren't missing. They're hiding out. And I'm pretty sure they're turning tricks in the townhouse. I'm goin' out there tomorrow and have a talk with 'em, or at least with Karen. See if I can find out what she's up to."

"Okay. Let me get on the computer here. Find out what I can about this Downs character. I'll get back to you before you leave."

"Great! Thanks, Jean."

While I waited for her return call, I started writing a first draft of the report I was going to give Danielle. I wrote down everything I'd just told Jean and started polishing it up when she called me back.

"Wha'd yuh find out?" I asked.

"First off, Downs is the guy's middle name. First name's Velma, if you can believe it. Last is Ratliff. V. Downs Ratliff, what he goes by. Born and raised in Jackson, Mississippi. Got a sheet. Been in trouble since he was a juvenile just like Routh. No way you can find out anything about that. Those records are sealed. Besides, they're in Mississippi. Unlike Routh, his juvy bust had to be something more serious than joyriding in his daddy's car. That's why the records are sealed. He never got his high school diploma, and he didn't take the G.E.D. Dropped out and moved to Los Angeles. When he was only eighteen in 1979, he was arrested for importation of a controlled substance for sale. It was pot. Did two years at San Luis Obispo. Took some college level classes in prison. Got enrolled in the junior college down there when he got paroled. Cuesta College. Special program for ex-cons. Transferred to U.C. Santa Cruz. That's where he met Darryl Routh. And you were right about his skin color. I've got two shots of him here. One's a mug, the other's a prison shot. I think he's an albino. His race is listed as Caucasian. I don't think there's a separate classification for albinos. The car is registered to Darryl Routh."

"Wow! What a record! Okay, Jean, here's the deal. I'm goin' up to campus and talk to Stein again. See if I can get any more information out of him. 'S afternoon I'm go'n'a call the number from the ad in the paper. Make an appointment for tomorrow afternoon. See if I can find out what's goin' on. Maybe get her to call her aunt and her parents so they'll all stop worrying about her. 'Less those two guys're there when I get there, I shouldn't have any more dealings with 'em."

"I certainly hope that's true."

"I'll let you know what I find out."

Sixteen

It was almost eleven o'clock when I got into my ten-year-old Honda Civic and headed up to campus again. Cruising up Walnut Avenue by the high school, I noticed a maroon Blazer two cars behind me. By the time I got to the corner of Mission and Bay, I realized it was a tail. He stayed two cars back all the way up Bay. The distance was enough that I couldn't make out what the driver looked like or what the license number was, but at one point I saw that it was a vanity plate. I got the green light at Nobel Drive; he got the red. I caught the red at High Street, and by the time it turned green, he was coming up behind me. He made the left turn behind me on High Street as I drove toward the west entrance to the U. There were no other cars on the road, hence, none separating us, but he kept his distance.

I kept my eye on him in the rearview, and when we were about halfway between the arboretum and the west entrance, the Blazer suddenly accelerated and was coming at me fast. A quick look in the mirror told me Downs was behind the wheel. My only advantage in this situation was maneuverability, so before he could climb right up on my bumper and start pushing me, which is what I thought he had in mind, I cramped my wheel hard right and my car went into a turnout. Luckily there was one there when I needed it, and since I was still doing the speed limit, the maneuver worked handily. He was doing a good fifteen miles an hour over the limit, so when he tried to follow me, he was going too fast and his truck was so big and clumsy that he didn't quite make it. Instead he went crashing through a wire fence, glanced off a tree, doing some really bad damage to his left front wheel, and came to rest under the tree.

My heart was pounding; adrenaline flooded my system. I shifted into reverse, and as I got back out onto Empire Grade, I checked the Blazer's plate: TRIX. Downs got out. He didn't look like he was hurt, not that I would've done anything about it if he were, so I drove up to the west entrance and on to Stein's office.

As I approached his open door, I could hear a one-sided conversation going on. He was on the phone when I entered, talking about some event that was coming up on campus. The call only lasted another minute or two, and then he hung up.

"So, how might I be of further assistance to you Mr. Lefevre?"

He didn't seem nonplussed or in any other way confused by my second appearance at his door. After what Charles had told me he'd seen the night before, I knew he knew more than he was telling me but wasn't quite sure how to get it out of him, or even could get him to open up. My one advantage was that knowledge. It was a warm day so his jacket with the leather elbow patches was hanging on a rack by the door. He was still wearing a tie, but his sleeves were rolled up.

"Come on, Doc. You can cut the crap with the formalities and start tellin' me what yuh really know about Karen Babbit. The real story."

"The real story?" He *was* good, and articulate, too, but there was some hesitation. "I do not believe I know what you are talking about."

"You were seen with her last night."

If anything, the good doctor didn't have a poker face. The façade he'd put up seemed to dissolve and disappear before my eyes. I knew then that I had him.

"You still married, Doc, or you just wear that ring for the sake of appearance?"

"Don't call me that! My name is Dr. Stein," he said, as he got up and closed and locked the door. He was clearly flustered. "What in heaven's name are you talking about?"

"Oh, please! You know exactly what I'm talkin' about."

"You cannot prove anything."

"Oh, God! Give me a break, man! You think I can't prove what I know to be true."

"What do you know?"

"You just don't get it and never will. I know you saw Karen last night, and it wasn't for any academic counseling. She dropped your class. Did you tell her that her people are looking for her? Probably not. You're pathetic."

And with that I unlocked the door and headed out to my car. I drove to the east entrance to get off campus, so I didn't see whatever came of Downs and his little "accident." I'd look him up later, have more than a little chat with him.

Even though I wouldn't need him, I'd bring Charles along. He'd enjoy watching me finish the job he'd started in the parking lot. What jerks these guys were!

It was after noon when I got back to my place. I called Charles at his office.

"May I speak to Charles Van Houten please?"

"May I tell him who's calling?"

"Jack Lefevre."

"Thank you, Mr. Lefevre. Please hold."

"What's up?"

"I'm goin' after that pasty-faced asshole who attacked Lil. He tried to run me off the road up on Empire Grade 'bout an hour ago. Wan'a go?"

"Are you kiddin'? I wouldn't miss it. Tell me when and where, and I'll be there. Need some help?"

"Not really. You already got your piece of this asshole. Now it's my turn. I just thought you might like to come along and watch."

"I would indeed."

"We'll do it tonight. Eight o'clock, room 214, Saint George. We're go'n'a knock on his door."

"The direct approach."

"You got it, buddy. Wan'a meet me here at my place? C'n walk up there from here."

"See yuh at a quarter till."

He hung up. Then I called the phone number of the massage want-ad in the paper.

"Hi, this is Natalie. How may I help you?"

Her voice was soft and smooth with a dreamy quality. Very sexy. All right! Not much doubt I was talking to Karen Babbit.

"Yes, I'd like to get an appointment for a massage. How much, and what's included?"

"It's a hundred dollars, and I really don't want to go into detail on the telephone, but I can tell you that you'll get your money's worth. Would you like to make an appointment?"

"Yes, I would. You available tomorrow at noon?"

"Yes, and you are?"

"Jack."

"All right, Jack. I've got you scheduled for twelve noon tomorrow. The address here is 925 Chanticleer, unit four."

"I'll see you then."

We broke the connection. I spent the next couple of hours bringing my report up to date, and then at three-thirty low tide, I went surfing.

Seventeen

Charles knocked on my door at a quarter to eight on the nose, looking like his usual relaxed self. I was refreshed and loose after my surfing session.

"Ready to go kick some ass?" I asked.

"You bet. Let's go."

We got to the Saint George ten minutes later. There were five people sitting on the couch and easy chairs in the lobby watching T.V. Some of them didn't look much different than the vagrants on the Mall. We went up the marble staircase to the second floor and to room 214. I slipped on the gloves I wore for such situations. Ratliff, still bruised and black-eyed from Sunday, opened the door so quickly that it was as if he were expecting somebody. Charles was standing against the wall, and Ratliff couldn't see him. Before he could register who I was, I caught him with a stiff left jab to the nose, right on the button. It was about the only part of his face that Charles hadn't already smashed up. He staggered back, nose gushing blood, and before he could get his balance, I caught him square on the jaw with a right cross. He went down for the count. While all of this was going on, Charles stepped quietly into the room, closing the door behind him.

"So, *Velma!*" I said sarcastically when Ratliff regained consciousness and was sitting on the floor propped up against the wall. His nose had bled down onto the front of the Pendleton style shirt he was wearing earlier when he tried to climb up on my rear bumper, and he rubbed his, by now, black-and-blue jaw where I'd hit him. "What's your part in this Karen Babbit business?"

"Fuck you, asshole!"

His defiance was palpable, but he had such a high voice, and the weakness of it made his current circumstances comical. He struggled to get to his feet, but Charles stepped over, and without any effort, pushed him back into his seated position on the floor against the wall.

"You'll get up when I say you c'n get up, fuck face, so just keep your seat for now," I said.

There was a knock at the door. Charles stepped back and opened it. Routh was standing there, and when he saw what was going on, he tried to turn and run, but Charles was quicker than he was. He reached out, grabbed him by the collar and dragged him inside and closed the door.

"Glad you could join us," I said. "Maybe *you* can tell us what's goin' on with Karen Babbit."

"I don't know what you're talking about."

He looked scared, but his pal, bloody nose, black eye and bruised jaw in the bargain, still looked defiant.

"So that's your story and you're sticking to it?

Yuh wan'a play it that way? Okay. I know what's goin' on, and I'm go'n'a take it to the end. And you two assholes aren't go'n'a get in my way. So, don't even think about it. And if either of you even so much as look at me or my neighbor again, I'm go'n'a hurt you so bad that your whole damn family's go'n'a' feel it."

I grabbed Routh by the collar and pushed him straight into Ratliff. They sprawled on the floor, blood everywhere. Charles and I turned and walked out.

Eighteen

After my bike ride on Tuesday, I spent the rest of the morning getting ready for my appointment with "Natalie" at noon. I studied and memorized a list of questions I made up to ask her when I got to the address on Chanticleer. Then I updated my report to the present and put it in a manila envelope. I'd finish it when I got back to the office after I talked to Karen.

At eleven-thirty, I drove out to Live Oak and got to the townhouse at quarter to twelve. I parked a little way away near Brommer, so it took me a few minutes to get there from the car.

I rang the bell, and after a short wait, Karen Babbit opened the door. Standing before me was the beautiful young brunette I'd seen in the picture Danielle had given me of herself and her niece. Karen's only slightly-made-up indigo eyes sparkled with delight. Her smile was infectious, and it highlighted the dimple in her chin. She looked voluptuous in her low-cut tube top with exposed midriff. Her red miniskirt was so tiny that it just barely covered her delta. Fishnet hose defined her shapely legs that were also accentuated by stiletto heels.

"Aren't you the handsome one," she said holding the door open. "You must be Jack. I'm Natalie. Won't you come in?"

I entered a well-appointed living room with a staircase going up the wall on the right side, directly opposite the front door. Another young woman, dressed similarly, was lounging on a sumptuous sofa along the wall opposite the staircase. She had long, blond, curly hair and the same come-hither smile as Karen.

"I'm Jasmine," she said. "You can have both of us for a hundred fifty."

"I don't think so," I said with what I hoped was an "aw shucks" grin. "In fact, I don't think I'm go'n'a have either of you."

Their smiles disappeared in the blink of an eye.

"Wha'da yuh mean?" said Karen.

"I know your names aren't Natalie and Jasmine. Karen and Rebecca is more like it. I even know your last names. Babbit and Ginsberg. Am I right?"

"Say, what is this?" Rebecca said.

"Yuh know, Karen," I said without acknowledging Rebecca's question, or even her presence, for that matter. "Your parents and your aunt Danielle are worried about you. My name's Jack Lefevre, and I'm a private investigator hired by them to find you."

"Oh, no," she said in a withering voice. "I knew I should've kept in touch with them, but Rebecca and Darryl said it would be better not to for now."

"*Natalie!*" Rebecca said. "You don't have to tell him anything."

"So why didn't you?" I said, still not paying any attention to Rebecca, and focusing directly on Karen.

"Well, you know I haven't chosen the most reputable of professions."

"No kiddin'."

"It's not as bad as you think. It's sex work, and it's a new way for liberated women to earn a living while at the same time being instructional—I'm a sex educator—and having fun. Not to mention, the money's very good. I've got two more dates this afternoon."

"Sex work. That what you call it? What about school? You planning on finishing your education?"

"Natalie, why are you telling him all this? You don't owe him any explanations. Don't say another word."

"I know, but if we ever expect to have legitimate careers in this field, we need for people like him to understand what we're doing and why we do it," she said to Rebecca, then, to me, "we're just getting ready to make the next move. Last week we got an interview with the Mitchell brothers at the O'Farrell Theater. We have a manager, and he showed them a film that Jasmine and I performed in together. We met Nina Hartley at the interview. She's a rising star in the adult film industry. The money's even better in porn than in prostitution."

Suddenly, I remembered the expensive, professional photo and video equipment in Routh's room at the Palomar.

"And as far as school is concerned," she continued, "I'm planning on transferring to San Francisco State in the spring once we get established in the industry."

"Look, ladies." This was the first time I acknowledged Rebecca's presence. "I don't really care what you do or what your motives are. I just think you, Karen, ought to let your family know where you are. They're worried about you."

"I was planning on telling them soon. I just need a little more time."

"Yuh have to know that I'm go'n'a be telling Danielle pretty soon here."

"Oh, God!" Rebecca said.

"I know," Karen said. "It was just a matter of time. I'll have to do it sooner or later."

"Sooner is better. All right, ladies. I'm leaving here now. I found out what I needed to, and now I'm go'n'a finish my report. I strongly advise you, Karen, to call your aunt Danielle and let her know you're all right."

"I will," she said without looking at me. She seemed genuinely sorry for not having done so.

As I walked back to my car I thought about the situation. Neither of those women seemed particularly sorry or apologetic for what they were doing to earn money, and Karen did give a pretty decent explanation. Who was I, or anybody for that matter, to judge their behavior? They both seemed happy, well adjusted. They were simply looking on it as work, gainful employment. And who knows? With all this video and D.V.D. technology going on these days, pornography may be the wave of the future. It might become acceptable.

They reminded me of Renata, a married woman I got involved with ten years ago when I was taking a legal studies class up at the U. I was engaged to be married at the time and really shouldn't have fallen for her wiles. Anyway, as I was falling in love with her, she claimed to have "screwed" fifty guys before me. That was a warning that I should've recognized from the beginning, but I didn't because my little head was thinking for my big head. The bottom line was that Renata, like these two women, was perfectly well adjusted. She simply liked having multiple sex partners, and she looked at it all as a learning experience both for her and the guys she "screwed." The only difference between her and these two women was that the latter two were making money at it.

Nineteen

I took a quick cruise down to Cowell's to check the surf on my way home. Low tide wasn't happening till four-twenty. At a quarter to one there wasn't much breaking, but there was a swell, and it looked like it was going to start picking up in a little while. There were some pretty decent sets coming through at Indicators, the next break out. It was a beautiful day, and there weren't many surfers in the water, so I decided to go out. I drove back to the house and called Danielle.

"Have you found Karen?"

"As a matter of fact, I have. Talked to her about an hour ago."

"Oh, boy! You'll never know how happy that makes me! When will I be able to see her?"

"Look. Why don't yuh come on over here when you get off today, and you can see my complete report? We'll talk then."

We set up an appointment at my office for a quarter to five. I typed up the last page of the report and put it in the envelope with the rest of it.

Then I went surfing. I was in the water by

three and stayed out till just before low tide. When I got home, I took a shower, had a snack and waited for Danielle. I turned on the T.V. and watched a little bit of the pre-game show for the A's/Giants World Series game. Danielle knocked on the door at fifteen to five on the nose.

"Come in," I said holding the door open for her. "How're yuh doin'?"

"Not bad. I hope your report's going to make me feel better."

"Probably not."

We sat down at my desk, and I handed her the manila envelope. She spent about five minutes reading what I'd written, and then the questions came.

"So, it's true. Karen's a prostitute."

"'Fraid so. And she seems happy doing it, but her and her friend Rebecca's next goal is to get involved in adult movies. She talks about it like it's some sort of instruction—sex education for the liberated woman."

"Does she have some sort of time frame when she plans to tell her family?"

"Oh, yeah. I think you'll be hearing from her soon. She thinks, and rightly so, that none of you will approve of her career choice. She wanted to get established in the adult film industry before she let you know. I'm pretty sure that timeline has changed. I wouldn't be surprised if you heard from her tonight."

"Well, Jack," she said. "Right now, I'm going home, and I'm go'n'a watch the ball game with Jason. Won't even think about this tonight."

"Good idea," I said.

Oh, Hard Tuesday

Then the earthquake hit and Danielle went home. I secured my property and went over to Lil's and helped her out. Then I went over to the Mall and saw the guys digging in the rubble of Ford's department store. One of them saw me coming and said,

"Give us a hand here! There're people underneath all of this!"

So, I pitched in, and as we got the bricks removed, I could see that it was two women, one older with short gray hair, and one younger with long black hair. A couple of the guys were trying to find a pulse on them.

"Hey! This one's still alive!" said the guy checking the pulse on the younger one.

"This one's gone," the other guy said, moving over to the live one.

At that point all of us started helping to clear debris away from the younger woman. As we got the dirt and rubble off of her, I saw it was Karen Babbit.

Twenty

It took some time to get Karen clear of the debris, but we finally did. She stopped breathing at one point, and a couple of us administered C.P.R. She started breathing again.

There was no phone or electricity, so we just had to wait to get help. It finally arrived in the form of an ambulance that came in on Cathcart Street. The E.M.T.s checked both women's vital signs, and they confirmed what we all already knew. The older woman was dead; Karen was alive, but unconscious. Nevertheless, they took both women away on stretchers. I went back over to stay with Lil and get ready for the night.

We didn't have any phone or electricity for four days after the quake, and general confusion prevailed for the next month. Danielle checked on Karen at Dominican Hospital daily during that time. She picked me up on Fridays, and I went with her. Karen remained comatose until Thanksgiving Day. Amazingly, she hadn't sustained too much facial damage, and that was starting to heal as time passed. She was still the striking beauty she'd been before the quake.

Oh, Hard Tuesday

When she finally did open her eyes, she had a blank stare. I saw her the next day, and she didn't recognize me at all, but she seemed to have vague recollections of her aunt Danielle and her parents. As time passed, she did get better, but I don't think it ever got above seventy percent. The last time I saw her a year and a half after the quake, her speech was still slightly slurred, and she really wasn't making connections, but she did know Danielle and her mom and dad by then. She had a vacant look in her eyes, but her stunning beauty was intact.

The End

1991-2019

About the Author

Jerome Arthur grew up in Los Angeles, California. He lived on the beach in Belmont Shore, a neighborhood in Long Beach, California, for nine years in the 1960s. He and his wife Janet moved to Santa Cruz, California in 1969. These three cities are the settings for his ten novels and one memoir.

CPSIA information can be obtained
at www.ICGtesting.com
Printed in the USA
FSHW012323140920
73779FS